DoveTales

One World, One People

Patricia Jabbeh Wesley, Ph.D., Guest Editor

2019 DoveTales Anthology

An International Journal of the Arts

Published by Writing for Peace

DoveTales, an International Journal of the Arts
"One World, One People"

DoveTales is published
by Writing for Peace
P.O. Box 270908
Fort Collins, CO 80527.

Email: editor@writingforpeace.org.
www.writingforpeace.org

A note on photographs and art: Unless otherwise indicated, photographs and art are independent of writings published in DoveTales. Photographs and art do not illustrate incidents, events, or characters depicted by writers; writings are not intended to describe incidents, events, or characters depicted in the photographs and art.

Front Cover:
"Entwined"
Carmel Mawle

ISBN: 978-0-9891206-7-8 Print Edition

Printed On Demand by Ingram Sparks

DoveTales

Contents

POETRY

FICTION

NONFICTION

ART & PHOTOGRAPHY

YOUNG WRITERS

Editor's Note:

Dear Friends,

"If you want to go quickly go alone, but if you want to go far, go together."

"A bundle cannot be fastened with one hand."

These are two African proverbs that come to mind when I think of our theme for the first online issue of Dove-Tales: An International Journal of the Arts. Our theme, "One World, One People," came to mind as I thought of where we are today in the world of multiple conflicts, threat of war, violence, conflicting messages from world leaders on what peace is or keeping the peace is, and a complete lack of unity on how to take care of the less fortunate of our one world. There is a new, quiet war against immigrants and migrants around the world and a new rise in anti-immigrant sentiment around the world, the apparent inability of world leaders to fight for peace, and the lack of agreement by the world body of leaders on the effects of growing catastrophic climatic changes. What was once a world united in protecting us from war and disaster no longer is, and from Europe to Africa, from the Americas to the ends of the earth, there is an unsettling fear that we have forgotten how to protect the world as a people and as a world body.

This edition of DoveTales is a call on all of us writers and readers to remember that we are indeed one people. No matter our skin color or our geographic locations, we are "one world, one people." DoveTales: An International Journal of the Arts has always been about the beautiful, sometimes sad or scarred, stories from around the world—about writing for peace, and speaking peace even in the midst of world disunity or calamity. No matter what political leaders say or do, this new online edition, as with past print editions, is a reminder that we are one world and one people, and we must never forget that.

John Donne's Meditation XVII, that powerful 1623 poem, captures this vision embedded in our theme as much as the African proverbs above do. Here in this fourth stanza of one of the most popular pieces of this great author, Donne admonishes us:

> "No man is an island entire of itself; every man
>
> is a piece of the continent, a part of the main;
>
> if a clod be washed away by the sea, Europe
>
> is the less, as well as if a promontory were, as
>
> well as any manner of thy friends or of thine
>
> own were; any man's death diminishes me,
>
> because I am involved in mankind."

Yes, we indeed are "One World, One People," even when it doesn't seem that way. One nations' or continents' destruction is destruction for the rest of us. As Donne said in so many words in Meditation XVII so long ago, we are affected by one another in every way.

This theme is most fitting for the first online issue of DoveTales: An International Journal of the Arts because now our contributors and readers around the world can have access to the journal they love so much without the limitation that a print edition forces on us—whether they have a small phone, an iPad, a tablet, or a computer. Many of our readers around the world did not have access to the print editions of the past, a problem now solved in the decision to bring this great journal to the world.

As the African proverb says, "If you want to go quickly go alone, but if you want to go far, go together," DoveTales: An International Online Journal of the Arts, is going far, and as we of "One World, One People," move forward into the future, we must "go together." I also believe that if we go together, we will go quickly since we will pull one another up higher as we go far into the future. And again, as another African proverb says, "A bundle cannot be fastened with one hand," we intend to continue this new vision of reaching our worldwide audiences and contributors wherever they are. Together we will fasten the "bundles" that are scattered in our world, whether they are children forced to migrate with parents from whom they will be separated in their new free world, or whether they are immigrants or migrants being attacked in Europe, parts of Africa, in America or even in Asia, whether our bundles include writing about the changing climate conditions that have become catastrophically disastrous for our one world people, or whether those bundles limit women in the world—through rape and the abuse of children and women—we are going "far" and going "together" as "one world, one people."

If "a bundle cannot be fastened with one hand," we know that a bundle also cannot be loosened with one hand, and if no woman/man is an island entire in herself/himself, then together we will tie the bundles with all our hands, or loosen all the bundles that hinder our one world. We will go far beyond our own expectations first, whether we write about the things that plague our world or the things that unite us.

We are excited about this beautiful first online edition with an array of amazing and diverse poems, fiction and nonfiction pieces, photography, and art by contributors from around the world. This issue is the Contest edition that includes works by the Young Writers Contest winners from around the globe, many who are writing in English as a second language. Congratulations to our winning authors and to all of our contributors. Also, in this issue are the first set of poems from the small West African country of Liberia, with young writers between the ages of 18 and 21, all publishing their first poems ever. DoveTales, An International Journal of the Arts has since 2013, drawn together writers from across the globe, whose vision is to forge peace through the pen, and this edition is no different. Some of our contributors include the finest writers in the US and around the world, and to them we are grateful.

Thanks to all of you, our audiences around the world, contributors, editors, fellow advisers, and our Managing Editor, Carmel Mawle, who has tirelessly and patiently put up with me. Finally, as our leaders struggle to find peace in the midst of turmoil and chaos, may we write peace into the minds not only of our youth, but to all of the world. As One World, One People, let us dig deep into ourselves for what makes us one. Let's stand together as the bundle that is fastened one to another since none of us is an island. And tied together, we can "go far." Celebrate with us this first online edition and celebrate one another as one world, one people.

Thank you.

Patricia Jabbeh Wesley, Ph.D.
Guest Editor

My Mother's Tale:
for My Mother

She stood there on a Saturday morning,
painting a mental picture in her mind,
watching the heavy downpour
that had begun the day before
but still didn't seem to be near the end.

Our bag of rice is empty, and if you know,
you know that you shouldn't play
with Liberian people's rice business.
In this Liberian household,
we eat country rice only.
She imagines the hassle she'll go through
to "find car." On this rainy, cold,
wet Saturday morning, she thinks
of the beans she cooked on Thursday,
the one Baby Arkoi likes, but didn't enjoy
because she likes it with country rice
not the imported *nyanmanyama.*

She imagines Gorbachev market, Red-Light,
where the *zogoes* hustle rain or shine,
where there is mud, red, thick, stinking mud.
She imagines the *portor, portor,*
but like a hen who has waited for the rain
that refuses to cease, like a hen,
that keeps her children warm
under her wings while her heart breaks
from watching them starve,

like a hen, that goes into the rain ignoring
the cold, searching for the last rice grain,
Mama Arkoi put on her boots, got herself ready,
and ran through our flooded yard, into the rain.
Looking for rice for us her chicks,
my wonderful mother.
It's Sunday morning, and it's raining still,
Rev. Arkoi looks out the window,
pointing at the chickens in the rain.

Our *Desse*, my *Esika* though from another world,
relates to that country chicken
more than *Mawein*, the Lorma people's stranger,
more than *Sumowuo*, a son of the soil,
Mama Arkoi looks at the chickens, and smiles
and then laughs, her laughter so alive
and sweet like the melodies of her people,

like the Lingala songs from her people,
the Congolese people, who know how to sing
so well, songs I don't understand, but try to sing.
She laughs, thinking about yesterday's
trip to Red-light Market.
Looking out the window, she says, "I remember."

One World, One Body

By Pilar Rodriguez Aranda, Adviser

It's always a challenge to choose one's own poem, or write one, given a certain theme. For this issue, it was particularly difficult for me to choose one text (although I did at the end), and at some point I thought it'd be easier to find a Mexican or Latin American poet who had already reflected this issue's theme: "One World, One People." But, once I had embarked on this, I realized I'd gotten "lost at sea," an immense sea of literature. So, it was pretty much aleatory that I ran into a poem by Pablo Neruda, its title caught my attention.

Neruda was a communist Chilean Nobel prize winning poet, who, at 34 years of age was already considered Chile's greatest poet. Thanks to his prestige, he was able to save almost 2,000 Spanish patriots who were in French internment camps; by leasing a boat ("The Winnipeg") with the help of the president of Chile, and other supporters like the Quakers, the Spanish migrants were all transported to safety. Neruda would always proclaim that the Winnipeg had been his "most beautiful poem." This anecdote shows Neruda's experience and commitment for those who are forced to migrate, recognizing, as the theme of this issue asserts, that we are in one world, and therefore, we should all be one people.

Attempting a version of Neruda's poem, without being a scholar on his work, could seem intimidating, but one must allow oneself to perform these exercises. Translating the masters is truly a wonderful school, unending and revealing. As writers, translators, word-slingers, our responsibility is to develop our vocabularies, learn and listen permanently and insistingly, always thinking of "the other," the one who will be reading our words; how can we impact with honest emotion rather than with mere argument? What kind of images will we choose to create and follow in an attempt to engage in communication, and transcend beyond the soliloquy? What words will we choose to do so, not by telling, but by showing and feeling?

Questions are infinite, and writing needs them because, just like life, it is an interminable process of decision making, of taking sides, yielding, assuming and committing. The greatest writers are passionate, usually very political people; those who are apathetic rarely leave a mark on us. Neruda's choice of words, takes the readers, seamlessly, from the realm of nature to the realm of universal empathy, as he starts to bestow emotions to the flock, and highly praise the process by which all the birds become one, just like the feathers conform the wing, just as we all are "joined...by blood, by thirst, by hunger...by the erotic urgency of life."

After reading and translating such a powerful and subtle (and long) poem, I wasn't sure if I should submit mine, but I decided I'd take advantage of DoveTale's digital issue, because I felt my poem touches upon another aspect of who we are as one people. As Neruda says of the birds, whether we do it consciously or not, we humans are all one huge body: we are birds and rocks; feet and bridges; hands and bodies. We are interconnected. Even if we all assume different roles, we can relate to the other's role, accept our divergences, and build on them. The path we lead, perhaps, as the poet would suggest, needs to be based on instinct, nature, and trust.

Pablo Neruda

Migration

ALL day long a line and another line,
a squadron of feathers,
a ship
throbbing in the air,
crossing
the small infinite
of the window from where I search,
interrogate, work, stalk, wait.

The tower of the sand
and the marine space
are joined there, resolving
the song, the movement.

Above, the sky opens up.

So it happened like this: straight, acute,
throbbing, they went by
to where? Towards the North, towards the West,
towards the clarity,
towards the star,
towards the rock of solitude and salt
where the sea dismantles its clocks.

It was an angle of birds
led
such latitude of iron and snow
advancing without truce
on its rectilineal path:
it was the devouring rectitude
of an obvious arrow,
the numbers in the sky traveling
to procreate in line
by urgent love and geometry.

Pilar Rodriguez Aranda, Adviser

I insisted on looking until losing
my eyes and I have not seen
but the order of flight,
the multitude of the wing against the wind:
I saw serenity multiplied
by that transparent hemisphere
crossed by the obscure decision of
those birds in the firmament.

I saw nothing but the path.

Everything remained celestial blue.

But in the crowd of birds
straight to their destiny
a flock after another drew
triangular
victories
joined by the voice of one single flight,
by the unity of fire,
by blood,
by thirst, by hunger,
by cold,
by the precarious day which cried
before being swallowed by night,
by the erotic urgency of life:
the unity of the birds
flew
towards the toothless black coasts,
dead crags, yellow islands,
where the sun lasts longer than its journey
and develops in the warm sea
the plural pavilion of sardines.

On the rock assaulted
by the birds
the secret got ahead of itself:
rock, humidity, excrement, solitude
will ferment and under the bloody sun
sandy creatures will be born
who someday will fly back
towards the hurricane-light of the cold,
towards the Antarctic feet of Chile.

Now they cross, populating the distance
barely moving their wings in the light
as if joined by a single heartbeat,

they fly without letting go

of the migratory

body

divided and dispersed

on land.

Over the water, in the air,
the innumerable bird goes flying,
the vessel is one
the transparent ship
builds unity among so many wings,
with so many eyes opened towards the sea
that it is one single peace crossing
and only one immense wing moving.

Bird of the sea, migratory froth, wing
of the South, of the North, wave wing
cluster spread by the flight,
hungry multiplied heart,
you will arrive, big bird, to shell

the necklace of delicate eggs
hatched by the wind and nourished by the sands
until a new flight multiplies
once again life, death, development,
wet cries, hot excrement, and
again be born, depart, far away
from the wasteland to another wasteland.

Far away
from that silence, flee, birds of the cold
to a vast rocky silence
and from the nest to the errant number,
arrows of the sea, leave me
the humid glory of the course,
the famed permanence of feathers
that are born, die, last and throb
creating fish by fish its long sword,
cruelty against cruelty its own light
and against-wind-and-sea, life.

**Translated by Pilar Rodríguez Aranda*

Puente

By Pilar Rodriguez Aranda

"Sólo el puente conoce el río,"
dijo Dante
escritor de Guadalajara

Ser puente...
No estar ni en un lado
ni en el otro
sino en ambos
Dejar que crucen otros
Mirar hacia abajo
El correr del agua
-sobre lodo, sobre piedras
Movimiento gris
verde, café, amarillo
Canto aullido susurro
A veces silencio

Debajo del puente
meses secos
invisible la muerte
como invisible la vida cruzan cientos
pies, pasos, voces
Y cree que va y viene
pero son otros tantos
son sus zapatos
resonando

Uno como puente
permanece
aferrado a un lado
y al otro
El puente escucha, une, calla

Sobre la espalda
nada que nos quiebre
Pasan los años
jóvenes y viejos

Pilar Rodriguez Aranda, Adviser

Reflejos sobre el agua
congelada en el invierno
su mirada
La arena, la tierra, el lirio
van cediendo
Nada es eterno

El puente no parece moverse
Pero cuánto tiene
por contar.

1992

Bridge

(Translated by the author)

"Only the bridge knows the river," said
Dante
a writer from Guadalajara

To be bridge...
Not on one side
nor the other
but on both
Let others cross
Look down onto
The water running
-over the mud, the stones
Moving gray
green, brown, yellow
Song howl whisper
Sometimes silence

Under the bridge
dry months
invisible death
as invisible the life
of the insect

Crossed by hundreds
feet, steps, voices
And believing it's coming and going
but it's the others
their shoes
resounding

As a bridge
one stays
clinging on to
one side and the other
The bridge listens, joins, is quiet

Over our backs
nothing to break us
Years go by
young and old

Reflections on the water
frozen in the winter
of their eyes
Sand, earth, lilies
are giving away
Nothing is eternal

The bridge appears not to move
But has so much
to tell.

1992

*

[Editor's note: The Neruda Foundation denied permission to publish the original poem. Here, we publish Pilar Rodriguez Aranda's beautiful translation, which we believe falls within the fair use statutes of copyright law. For more information on fair use, see "Code of Best Practices in Fair Use for Poetry, " by the Center for Media & Social Impact.

Free Me

Free me from your endless rumors.
I speak the way I do
because I was taught in school
that my subject and verb should agree.
And that's a rule.
I'm sorry, if you didn't pay much attention
in school, but don't dare tell me
I'm trying to speak seerees
or that I sound American.
I don't always have to speak colloquial
to prove I'm from LIB,
so, free me!

Free me from your bizarre stereotypes.
Don't question me being a Lorma girl
because I don't have a big backside
I know that you think that my "behind"
is flatter than a door
You think you're rubbing it in,
but you cannot because
I like being me.
Free me!

Free me from your ruthless gossip
Don't go explaining that I'm too young
to be a mother.
I was naive and lost, always in the wrong
places, with the wrong people,
but that's not your business.
You saw me... all the time
when I needed a hand to lead me.
You did not make it your business
to give advice.
Now, make it not your business
to gossip about my child and me.

Free me from your labels.
Yes, you say I'm a talkative,
but I have a right to contribute
to conversations.
so, don't dare tell me I like to fuller-place
Free me!

Free me!
I like my "sentimentality"
I like my slimness; I like my laugh,
the way I talk, and I like
the way I makeup my face.
I just love being me, and I'm never
going to fit the space
you've carved up for me.
So, free me!

Max Doesn't Know

in his veins thrums the blood of genocide, the strength of survivors, my grandson, with his bright blue eyes, doesn't know yet the costs his ancestors paid, how many died, blood spilled for gold, doesn't realize those shining beads he holds with his chubby hands are corn tears dropped, silvery as coins, growing like wounded miracles to mark the path to Oklahoma.

He doesn't know about the Guineamen, about human cargo, glistening black bodies broken in the holds, thousands thrown away like trash, thrashed and chewed by great gray Atlantic waves, their names written only in the foam still crawling up on to the shore.

He doesn't know about the Great Starvation, mass graves, mothers curled around babies they couldn't feed or save, unearthed outside Dublin, bones clicking like rosary beads beneath the cold white sky. He doesn't know about coffin ships, the dead dragged out on boat hooks, tossed overboard, dreams drowning in the cries.

More, he doesn't yet know of Dachau, or Auschwitz, the purging, flames of hate sending millions of souls plumed as smoke into the heavens. He can't know how long the smell of burning flesh lingers, how numbers tattooed in blue ink on pale skin scar, never really fade, imprinting forever deep, even into dna.

He doesn't know the bone wounding of hunger, the relentless drum of an angry fist, or the horrific insistence of crosses setting the night ablaze. He knows only the world through three year old eyes, that red car, this blue bus, his father's strength, his mother's loving touch.

I hold him in my lap, breathe in the ancestral light, the miracle of resilience, this child. In him, in every child, generations birthed into sight, but he doesn't know he is their victory. I pull him close, whisper, you are the persistence of hope. He lifts his eyes to me and in them, I see creation. I see every soul, and weep, realizing, he does, in the way of angels, in fact, know.

A Summer's Day

with old friends

Faces wear from the surface in,
worked by our lives' abrasive tips,

each decade scoring deeper skin,
around the eyes, beside the lips.

Yet spirits strengthen with the rub,
and alter from mere humanoid

to life beyond their mortal snub:
oh, seraphs of the sunny void!

The Calling

to Yoga Meditation, 1967

An elephant descends from heaven.
It steps down foursquare in your garden,
Sent by, it states in princely tones,
The Guiding Spirit of Creation
to speed you out of this circle of stones
onto the straight road of Salvation!

Presuming sun induced delirium,
you hoe ahead, soulfully dumb.

Renounce those beans! trumpets the beast.
Forswear your loamy downward passion!
The Lord desires you at His Feast!
Attend Him in the yogic fashion:
Muse on the thinnest goblet lip,
traced by the subtlest finger tip,
sounding the aural strains of Light!
Khrisna awaits you, day or night!

Beans trampled to a seeping wallow,
what's there to do? Start up and follow.

Realized

an Arhat of Buddhism

in Kelania, Sri Lanka

He slept the nights of youth
near unaware of sleeping,
new-fangled days ahead
his only goal in keeping,

until great sets of waves,
or a deadly poison snake,
reared into nightmare shape
to threaten him awake.

Disquieted, he sought
pure *Being*—that still spot
between the restive ways
of body, heart and thought—

and found a solace there
dreams could not overlay—
where venom and the crush
of death must ebb away.

'All This Is That'

from the *Upanishads*

The Energy that binds
our bodies to our minds
enjoins our lives; its bond,
once weakened, may respond
to willpower, nursing care,
fresh outlooks, ease, or prayer,
and keep its grip some time
beyond our parents' time.
It will, alas, unfix.

Forget the stones and sticks
once heaved at nothingness,
our anger in duress,
the honest pleasures gleaned
from knowing that we dreamed—
there is a Fusion quite
beyond our spoken metrics,
vital day or night,
from which lifetimes unfix.

Elaine Gerard

The human in me

I see in the mirror
above my bed
these bare breasts
dimpled in the cool
of my bedroom,
peaked in the purple
darkness,
where the lingerie
is stepped over,
a velvet pool of
shimmering black
nightie.
I see my soft belly
rise and fall
with each weary
soul breath,
I touch,
close my eyes
and I just
am a woman,
just for tonight,
where I lie
alone
in the silent bed,
a ticking clock
and the curtains
that flit and
undulate as slow
as the moon's
numbed path,
then slumber
and pass
into dreams where
I am merely human,
a touch of color,
the lips red
and the soul
so blue,
the bruises purple
and golden fade;

I drift above
in a hue,
a hum,
an invasion,
I fly above
my sincere landscape,
sewn with careless
stitches,
crazy quilt country,
where spiders watch
my every move,
the monster waits
behind a pillow,
and I fly on by
so unaware,
I sit on a cloud
and sing,
there is no body,
I am just a thought,
a feather,
pulled to the edge,
looking down,
a shapeless person
a paper bag,
arms and legs
and nothing
but me in between,
I smile and
fly into my night,
where magenta skies
and alizarin crimson
prairies full of
speckled dun horses
churn and stampede,
I fly into those skies,
here in the dream,
where I am human,
I am just the
essence
of a me.

Veronica Golos, Adviser

Who will speak these days, If not I, If not you?

–Muriel Rukeyser, The Speed of Darkness

it is the dead who bother—the body

their swirl their capsizing   my
their amputation of a word before it becomes
how they catch like a snag in the everything of weeks

how I re member the murdered
the dead with their excellent moans

their damp clamp of sentence

how many when the many accumulate like like like a
lifetime

those war-dead the ones who went the ones who didn't
the ones who never looked up

they crowd inside me so
I am
empty of

liver intestines the lovely kidney third finger i won't say
heart I won't

i stand in a room so empty it is empty of me

who will be the throat of these hours

trembling in their neutered time

how the kill is done who does it why it is done in
the heavy rain or the brittle battlefield or a place
so green it hurls its color at you or the rice or the
banana or that which calls forth a lake or desert
or mud or land grass sky cow duck child infant a
pregnant woman herself an alphabet or abacus or
something else something dwindled down to your
own odor

what war flows through
the shape of your body speaking its evidence

those dead lose words ambulance breath buffalo
chiffon clavicle conflagration cusp croon crocus
cobalt crisp café dandelion (dandy lion) delirium
dunes echo eyelash well i could go on and on and
on and perhaps that is it those words the dead
will never list or lisp or say perhaps its as simple
as that as deadly as catastrophic as calamitous as
enough as that

oh   and chrysanthemum

Carol Griffin, three poems

Oh Blue

(after Chagall's The Blue Violinist)

Oh blue I sing my tune with string and bow,
I float above the town and everyone below
looks up and rises too and there the moon
holds heaven like a gift– bouquets of joy
unfold for everyone, we all take wing
and growing tall and young each find a love.
My hands like birds kiss the world with song–
I play my violin with lighted brow,
the music into blue, all blue, beyond
the gate I open light for you above
the church with eyes turned skyward too.

I Am the Refugee Walking

I am the refugee walking,
I am the rebel loading the mortar.
I am the woman, ankles held,
I am the blinded men who have her.
I am the slave brought to my knees,
I hold the lash.
I am the queer locked up,
I am the jailer locked in.

With indigenous tribes I am on the rise!
I hold the permit to extract the oil.
I am the gathering voice, the cry!
I am the wall of brutal fear.
I am the one who prays for peace,
who does not have enough to eat.

I am this bleating heart,
this chest strapped with explosive,
this yearning love
unbroken
forgotten.

Carol Griffin

Gaia May Not Have Realized

Gaia may not have realized
Euclid's axiom that any straight line
can infinitely be extended
when she built the Great Barrier Reef,
but I suspect so. I think of coral growing
from the tiniest polyps creating
crusty circles about themselves–
they propagate any way they can,
releasing gametes simultaneously
at the full moon– no straight lines in sight.
Isn't that the way though? What delights
in shallow seas becomes life's work,
just as these inconsequential scribbles
may become an opus, or the cricket
whose song holds up the night sky.

Laurel Ilionia

One World, One People

Last night, in my dream,
black angels dancing, to and fro,
upon the downward stairs,
from the heavenly gate,
proclaiming a word the earth has never known.
I was blind and deaf
and could not see nor hear the angels.
Deep was I in earthly things

Until I heard them say,
Jesus is the son, the Lord,
and also Mohammed is the son, the Lord.
I trembled at the sight.
My ears kept blocking my hearing,
and I pretended it was a joke.

I could hear them saying aloud,
Jesus is black, Jesus is white.
Whatsoever you take him to be,
he is, and I was baffled, my mind lost itself,
trying to believe,
what my world never believed.
With fear, I heard the words of the angels,
who beheld me, stronger than true love.
And I could not resist their words.

I could hear them saying again,
We're the angels of truth and purity,
Fear not. For you're the chosen one.
Tell your world,
the truth, they never knew.

Oh, I replied, in a deep heavy voice,
I fear, they won't believe me.
And I will become a caricature.

My world kills the innocent for nothing.
Color, religion, luxury kills us.
In one voice aloud, they replied,
Go into the world.

Spread what you have heard. For our God (Allah) is with you.
Tell them, they are;
One world, one people.

I bowed my head and cried
With a pain filled voice, I said,
My world has been in darkness,
For these centuries.

I could hear them say, in a powerful voice,
Strong as the wind,
Go! Go!
You have no time to spare.

What We Say

Late autumn. The sun's
troubled: warm, dazzle,

or warn? I've yet to get
ready. All night

indifferent preparation
of frost. Elsewhere,

armies hard at work,
like the moon as we sleep,

suddenly on the move
if we looked, like it's always

had to be. At least,
that's what we say.

And in the morning,
the same—armies at work,

like the moon, like us,
unlocking our office doors,

tunneling through to afternoon,
with nothing else to say.

—first published in Why War, *Finishing Line Press, 2014*

Still

It all recurs for the maimed, how they remain,
or don't, atop the plots of the buried. Those
who could do something table the question.
They relax in the rocker of their certainty,
a war, any war, an abstraction that walls off
the bursting specifics. A twenty-something friend
found he'd deployed to sort body parts. Arrayed,
they'd survive the fever sweeping a land we
could never know. Welcomed by the white-blue
atrium of a foreign sky, he'd prowl his perimeter
until his duty tapped him. Then the oven-sun
would relight his nightmare, the categories
of bone and flesh his production line. What
achievement could signal his success? What
dream in the meantime could relieve raw nerve?
The perfect tour would end when he was still
in one piece, a nation's need ignoring the gore
behind the games, the horror nestling into
the still-living because still in one piece.

—first published in Tuck, *September 14, 2017*

D. R. James

Surreal Expulsion

—for Marjory Stoneman Douglas High School

Fourteen chairs loiter, emptied, no young bodies
adjusting for the next lesson, hand-raising,
class-clown antic, contemplative talk, pat show
of teen contempt, rhythm beaten with pencil, palm,
bouncing knee, jouncing heal, wise-crack, step
in the impossible problem never to be solved.
Instead, more of the same news, the same vows
taxiing the hellish hallways of feigned intention
but never taking off—the same dazed moments
of the dead. Perhaps their freed spirits now see
through the coal-black tunnel of some eternity
right into the next school's beehive of victims.
Perhaps they still shadow their three steady mentors
who stood staunch ground in the slow-motion flow
of high-speed ammo. The clip of names shoots holes
clean through law's callous gut—

Aaron, Helena, and Alex,
Carmen, Peter, Cara, Chris, and Meadow,
Scott, Alaina, Martin, Alyssa, and Nick,
Jamie, Luke, Gina, and "Guac" Joaquin—

whose roll call
claims only an absurd third of a minute, while
their totaled lives witnessed nearly 5 thousand
wheels of the moon through some 75 trillion miles.
But unlike the pull of that implacable moon,
the glib fever of 'prayers and condolences' can't
turn the tide of memory's radiating its fixed
fissures scored by shards of glass and bone.
Here, we're left to settle the moonscape of Too Late
for those whose expelled footsteps befuddle us.
And lauding immortality soothes no better. We
know we relax at our children's peril, run rash risk

of shoring up the open/closed-carry-frenzied fight,
take false hope in the bundles of white-washed **bills.**
Anthony Borges took five bullets to shield twenty
surviving friends, sacrificed his soccer stardom
because somehow *he* knew what he had to do.
His lacerated back and shattered femur scream
in a language we now must teach across America.

—first published in Bullets into Bells, *July 10, 2018*

Kerry Adamah Kennedy

Home

I hear the coconut trees moving against the wind
against my face,
of the pot-holes, the coal-tar down the avenue
of the sea, its silence that speaks of the weather,
its calmness in the wind.

Of the earth, they speak, telling of the blood
they've seen shed here on this shore, this Monrovia.
Of how men were killed, women, raped,
and babies were ripped from
their mothers' wombs.
Liberia, home, the Atlantic. Home.

Of the buildings, they speak, telling how
the buildings bore bullets to their sides,
of how it was home to child soldiers,
and how mothers were beaten, boys like me,
sodomized,
and turned into drug addicts.

Of the soil, they speak, telling stories of its richness,
of how crops would grow after the war.
And they speak of how we still thrive here
on cassavas, potatoes, watermelons,
pineapples, coconuts.
I hear the coconut trees speak to the wind,
this land, this still sweet land of liberty.

untitled

the sky is falling!, the sky is falling!
—Henny Penny

i'm the one
who's never home
when you knock
and if she is
when you don't
admits no one
black or white
living or dead

henny penny had many heads

i'm the trick i performed
long before i was born
like this poem written backwards
i'm the stunt that defies
i'm the cry to deaf eyes
whose only reply is
ashes ashes

the Lord moves in mysterious ways
and i am falling upwards

i'm the earth that turns
and fells me from its tree
i'm the ocean that slides from my shore
i'm a point as moved as any fixed mark
i'm the eyes of the dead potato
that finds it's way back in the dark

i'm the blood i give
but never give up
i'm the wine that flows outside the cup
i'm the truth inside the lie
i'm transparent butterfly

the Lord moves in mysterious ways
so why can't you or i?

i'm the play i'm writing without a plot
the word "forget" that i forgot
the regret that once escaped my lips
the mercy that hangs now round my hips
with the pull of gravity
the real of unreality
the all or nothing   the nothing of all
the indelible handwriting on the wall
that hummmms like a ghetto rhapsody

i'm the bum in the park who says less is more
the plexiglass sky of the invisible floor
the one who cries just outside your door

i'm the intimate stranger
whose smile will always hint of you
the Living Poem
the anonymous fingerprints of you
the enemy you befriend
whose soul can transcend you
the goodbye that may begin
but can never really end with you

i'm the saint   i'm the sinner
i'm the fish you ate for dinner
i'm the air growing thinner as i sigh
i breathe the breathless
my death is deathless
i'm the song i sing when i rise

i'm the altar kneeling
the all revealing   healing of the human kind
i'm the splinters i'm still peeling
from the cross i drag behind

i'm the mold and the molder
i'm the front-row-center season-ticket-holder
STEP RIGHT UP, FOLKS!
THE MYSTERY...THE STAR YOU'VE WAITED FOR!
i'm the protigee of the original sin
i AM the light i'm buried in

i'm the moth i'm the flame
i'm the prayers for the insane
i'm everywhere and nowhere
please remember my Name

Movin' On

Alone in my room I choke back tears
for the weeping world the sleeping world
the impoverished the sick the insane
I think of old debts the light years gone by
my memory down the drain

I used to hang
with hobos on park benches
ride the trains
with strangers through the trenches
listen to their stories in the rain
So sorry I'd say with a lump in my throat
while I wracked my brain for a solution
I prayed for evolution restitution
a revelation for the homeless the disillusioned
the ones whom only God could understand

Take my hand–I'd say–and let me hold you
Let me comfort and console you—
the brokenhearted the ones with whom love parted
the forgotten the absurd the unheard
Lord knows I could have done much more
Then a voice which haunts me still
whispered these words:

Forget the could have would have should have might have beens
the thousand and one excuses wearing thin
The promise of Heaven on Earth of Sun and Moon
was never hollow
Remember who you are a wondrous shining Miracle a star
Just do your best and all the rest will follow
You be Day I'll be Night
You be Love I'll be Light
Watch us spin in the dark !!
We're movin' on !

Antonia Alexandra Klimenko

With every breath   with every sigh
the living dead   the dying in my head   the unsaid
filters through this thin disguise   the white lies
the borders beyond the cosmos of your eyes
realizing the music unspoken between us
cannot be broken   The mark of your genius
something inside you was meaning to
stir a beautiful mind   the purr of the sublime
the Divine in you that shine Shine SHINEs !!!
The kinder kind was never defined
by subtraction division derision
or resting on their behind

There's something in the air
something rare   like I care
you can feel it
You can peel it off of every wall
see it rise and fall
spin it on the tip of your tongue
if you dare to
catch it as it flies   share it   watch it multiply
Everything in space   the human race   hummmms in the thick of it
Some of us too quick with it lose it   abuse it   refuse it
Others just plain sick of it
drown in the ocean of emotion
Call it what you will
it will change you   rearrange you

Energy synergy poetry
The acrobatics of that   can snap you to attention
the tension intention invention
the stunt of syllables   the pull of gravity
See my hand shake   hear my voice quake
Let it sail   let it sing
This moment is Everything!

Mystery comes unveiled   leaves a trail
Why not travel   take a chance   come unraveled
Let's be danced   like the stars

Plummet like a me-te-or
Feel the heat of the flame
or the beat on the street or
plant your feet on the summit of defeat
No blame

Why take a back seat
to the wide screen Cinema Paradiso
Why am I are you are we so
afraid of flying   of living of dying
of anticipation expectation deflation elation
Be in the air Be Fred Astaire
Bo Jangles Baudelaire
Come live your immortality
You're not some poor relation
you're a sensational spokenword vibrational
a Child of the Creational !

There's something you can't hide
in here out there inside
touches me   heals me
knows what is real what is true
can't sit down   or stand still
Everything in motion is a movie
is a spoof   is living proof   is through the roof
the sky the planets the ocean
The notion that we live we give forgive only to die
with fame instead of honor and devotion
is a celebrity game And so much locomotion
Stop going through the motions
Stay real Stay humble (just please don't mumble)

Those who stay with what they know
have nothing to show for it
Give up the ghost and go for it !
Feel the loss the pain the gain of your soul for it
If you find yourself rejected   be the metaphor resurrected
Move on move out and through the insanity

Sense all your senses   transcend ex-per-i-ences
Be the sequential your essential reverential potential
Move on from fear to love   what was I thinking of ?
Share your light   a blessed blessing
a transformation   a dance formation   a holy incantation
Pay it forward Be sublime ! Let it SHINE!

Take my hand and let me hold you
Let me comfort and console you
tell you all the things I never did before—
the ones with whom I've parted
the brokenhearted the forgotten the absurd the unheard
God only knows I might have done much more
Then a voice which haunts me still whispers these words

Forget the could have should have might-have-beens
the thousand and one excuses wearing thin
The promise of Heaven of Sun and Moon
was never hollow
Remember who you are—
a wondrous shining Miracle a star!
Just do your best and all the rest will follow
You be Day I'll be Night
You be Love I'll be Light
Watch us spin in the dark !!
We're movin' on !

You be Day I'll be Night
You be Love I'll be Light
Watch us spin in the dark
We're movin' on!

You be Day I'll be Night
You be Love I'll be Light
Watch us spin in the dark
We're movin' movin' on

Pensacola, Florida

Trudging through white sand
I don't notice the small indent
until my toe sinks into it—
a seabird's nest holding hatchlings
the size of dandelion seed pods
one wishes upon when one
stumbles upon one.
A barking "yip" from above
alerts me: a circling bird
with an odd reddish-blackish beak
like my pug's underbite
when he's dug a hole beneath
the fence and gets caught, his snort
and pouty lip wishing for
forgiveness, his eyes like the black
skimmer looking down on me.

Stranger in My Home

Inside these walls,
still water kills
scalloped waves.

Unexpected hushes
rush my eyes outside
where a blue heron waits.

You cannot embrace
awareness, a change
I cannot face

this hollow grave
filled sedate
as if we never met.

Will I escape
the chambers
of this strangeness?

I caress your
calloused hands
and am overcome

with memories
of lingering clinks, motor
hums from yesterday

it seems, the years
your mechanic hands
kept me afloat.

And now it's me
helping you even though
you don't know who I am.

Laurie Kolp

Forgiving Myself

Tonight, I fall asleep uncovered,
a sleep so deep I hear you
call my name and say hello.
Your words flow through me
pure as purest silk, loop to loop.
Our hands entwine.
A vague conundrum waves
through the aura you emit.
I wonder if your whisper
is my imagination,
your words persuasion
through a dream,
your essence chills.
You answer through my tears.
You say I must find a way
to let it go, find a way
to forgive myself.
Overtaken by an ache
I can't explain
drifting in the space
between us,
drifting to acceptance
I have no other choice
than to believe
that you are here.

Against All Odds

On the edge of life

I staggered, succumbing to the throes

of the divine and I began to wilt.

I was unaware that I was indispensable

knowing you had laden yourself equally

against all odds with the absolute essence

of my sole purpose with our sensuous

delectable union.

Against All Odds, photograph by Paula Dawn Lietz

The Explanation of A Lunar Eclipse

*For Wang Zhen Yi**

Silence.
Our speaking is deliverance of a scholar.
Then, less not, a woman.
Angle of Pythagoras sharp,
how equinoxes move.
Legacy on a string,
refrain of home,
son in mirror.
Silver setting moon
revolved,

Eclipsed.

Revolved
moon. Setting silver
mirror in sun.
Home of refrain –
string on a legacy,
move equinoxes, howl!
Harp, Pythagoras of angels.
Woman. A no less than
Scholar. Our deliverance Is speaking our
Silence.

**Wang Zhen Yi, an 18th century Chinese mathematician, astronomer, and poet. She died at age 29, left no children. She championed openly for gender equality in her lifetime.*

Unreliable Bystanders

– A Villanelle
Echoed were the reveries, escaping through the gate.
Unreliable bystanders whispered premonition –
We pedaled on these memories, about to be erased.

In '89, I was two. Bicycles rushed past the place
where the first day of the hunger strike asked for absolution.
Echoed were the reveries, escaping through the red gate.

In '99, we might have believed the daily spinning takes
of propaganda so set against the so called evildoers' indoctrination.
We peddled on these memories, made to be erased.

In '09, we've since learned not to meddle in each other's race.
Playing tourists in the nest built on the hubris of the revolution,
echoed were the reveries, escaped through the gate.

Could we ask for our tongues back or is it too late,
though could we comment above the firewall without repercussion –
Bellowing are the memories, afraid to be erased.

They scooped the body up like a puddle of jam, in my mother's face,
and stuffed it in their backpack, was a quiet dissolution.
Echoing are the reveries, escaping through the gate,
We pedal on these memories, made to be erased.

In memory of those who stood and lost 6/4/1989

Previously published in *The Remembered Arts Journal.*

may

you be lifted and surrounded
when you have a need of angels.

you be guided when you need the
moon, defying expectations.

justice be in your heart, for you
to freely share with those waiting.

the dark embrace you, keep you safe
from dreams that fear the light of day.

your children rise, God in their eyes,
knowing beauty waits in each day.

Matthew 19:13

If a child from some place like Florida,
Connecticut, or Colorado spoke to you,
said I'm tired of fearing violence,
we need to make a change, fuck this,
I can't vote yet, you need to bring change,
would you listen and act, be inspired,
or correct their choice of expletives,
deny the weight of their experience
when balanced by their tender age?

Think on this: What if they were yours,
if they were your brother's or sister's,
the children of your neighbors? Then?

What if a Dapchi girl, her life destroyed
by the so-called men of Boko Haram,
or a Yemeni brother and sister, orphaned
in the bloody rubble of an entire country,
came to you in search of sanctuary,
of a place to live without daily fear?
Would your religion welcome them,
would you embrace them at once,
or would you reject them, indifferent?

Think on this: They are yours.
They are your brothers and sisters.
They are your neighbors. Now what?

Lennart Lundh

Travel Journal #2

I remember Menominee, the reservation
where culture was for sale to tourists
at the weekly fire and tribal dance show.

I remember Bergen, the young American,
the young waitress, making an evening date
without a word in common except loneliness.

I remember Skansen, the glass blowers
and the costumed re-enactor docents
among the ancient red buildings.

I remember Hong Kong, the heads of oxen
and rope-bodies of headless snakes
for sale in the street market of Aberdeen.

I remember Danang, the fantail watch,
cradling a 12-gauge loaded with rock salt
while watching for swimmers with mines.

I remember Olongapo, kids begging,
the bar girls with the ready smiles,
and the meal at the Tokyo Hilton.

I forget the foreign tongues we spoke,
recall instead the commonalities
of daily people doing daily lives.

Begin

Just a single, rough, gray pebble,
as slight as a fingernail,

as tiny as a chip off a full-formed
wish, like an irritant wedged

between foot and sandal that could,
with much patience and persistence,

be saved and made into something
not big but on its way to small

then—eventually—larger: a statue, even,
holding up a torch. But this is not

about construction. There are a zillion
crushed stones as far as your peripheral

vision can see. And they are monochrome
and crowded. And they are as tall as twin towers

and wrap around the world. Face the wall.
Put your hands on it, your fingers a chisel.

It is a single, rough, gray pebble.
Start with that.

What Her Teacher Said about Nagasaki and Hiroshima

for D'Ann

She said what
she said was "If you look *she said was*
straight up into the horror of
was she said not sun
she said but bomb *was what she said* exploding suns,
exploding *decimating what she said was* us
she said what she said and your eyes *ours*
hers theirs what she said was
melting, melted would melt." And that is
everything is all
she *was what she* said *was*
is was *what* she *said* That is all
she remembers
she.

Previously published in *Sonic Boom.*

Found and Not Found

And when I lost you on the beach,
you were crossing only the threshold of the tide—

the Atlantic, not the Suchiate River or the Gulf—
and when discovered ten long moments later,

you raised your small hand and waved,
unaware of the terror in a parent's empty arms.

Go back, young one, to the life you never lost
to find those crying for the hand

that held them all night across the rough
crossing, only to lose them now in the dead

of night beside a border where patrols,
working the late shifts, grieve for their own

screaming children, much farther away
than the arm's length these small ones know

no longer. Lost child of mine
who grew up to flee far beyond

the search for sand dollars and shells,
hover over these unprotected strangers,

as tiny as you were
when the great ocean roared

its omens and you turned
quickly back into my seeking arms

aware only that someone
larger than you had desperately

called your name. Go now.
Do the same.

Columbarium

Why should I in insolence ignore
the microbial life of an old window
or anything that doesn't seem to hover into view?
All the dumb talk about original sin
just covers up what we do every day,
ignoring our vestigial gifts,
pretending not to say what we've already said
in a thousand other ways.
What is insolence but us beset
by what we think we need to stay alive?
I looked out of the window and saw
utility poles stitching Gaeia autopsied.
Nobody's going to forgive you
for the original sin of being you,
that's on you, you'll just have to find
other felons to hang out with
and some day you may even break out
of the squint of I into the blaze of you.
How are your grievances coming along?
Are they ready to rest under a paving stone?
Will you insist it have a name,
having taken your insolence with you
as if the fungi you ignored, the empires
in the cracks, the glances that gave birth
to chimera, the summons that shook
the marrow in your bones, were faery tales?
You ignored them too, the faeries,
the elementals, the possibility
that the one great adventure meant for you
waited in what you didn't know.
I've gone from I to you, did you notice?
And it was really all I was meant to do.

Filling My Water Bottle at Walgreen's

There are no lines, no buckets, no chatter
of daily gossip, no long dresses or vibrant
colors swirling in the wind, no baskets
balanced on heads, no children waiting
their turns while playing made up games,
no men with rifles or missiles, no animals
waiting for water, no chickens cackling,
no feet caked with dust,
no eyes staring into the long horizon, rheumy, blank,
no old women with lesions and old men with bent backs,
no place to sit, no story left to tell for who listens
anymore to how they took daughters and raped...
words running like overflow onto river banks, no women
nodding, knowing, having known the darkness.
No wails when done is done and done
                    in front of them.

No tongue-less sons, no sons left.
No effort to untangle a mangled day.
No flies swirling that defy a swat.

The no and no and no that gets lost in
the arc of water, gurgling, filling my water bottle.

The water is cold and clean, delicious and free.

Red Popsicles

We sit on the stoop.
It's too hot to do anything

else except to watch
Nelson jumping rope,

the girls swinging
double Dutch,

laughter
all the way to

stars we can't name,
dream on anyway.

Nelson's mother
brings us summer heaven:

red popsicles.

She sits, says little,
smiles at her teenage son

who loves the young
kids on the block.

She doesn't know
that in a week

neighbors will be late
for work

to see Nelson off
for service,

first in his family
to go to war

not one of us
imagining

how we will
line the still summer
streets,

for his return.

Her Greatest Silence

(In response to viewing The Greatest Silence
documentary film by Lisa F. Jackson)

I'm going to the Congo.
for 76-minutes,
for free, via a library rental DVD.

I watch shattered women
look
at the camera,
some numb
and some near tears.

They're on the screen.
I am on the couch.

I hear machetes,
guns,
blocks of wood,
were rammed inside
them:
2 yrs. old,
4 yrs. old,
15 yrs. old,
35 yrs. old,
and 80 yrs. old.

The rapists are there too,
though they deny wrong doing.
They hide their eyes with
sunglasses, drape their faces.
They smile, laugh.
And if the victims were their mothers,
their wives?, the interviewer asks.
They say, all for the Congo.

All for the Congo, its
diamonds, bauxite,
iron ore...
but women should be its
most precious jewel.
~
Raping women is a form
of reward,
pushing a sense of power
in those men.
Rape is a weapon of war,
quiet,
long lasting,
far reaching.
War becomes fought
through women's bodies.

Women
whose wombs make the nation.
Women whose hands
cook food. Women whose
heads carry water home.
Women whose backs strap
babies and rock them to sleep.
Those very women are raped,
        till their inner walls tear,
        beyond repair,
        and urine constantly drips
        from there, making them,
The victims, shamed and blamed.
Women of the Congo are cast out
from their homes because other men
forcefully entered them.
~
Women of the Congo suffer
and I sit here safe in my home.
I sit here warm, newly clothed,
and richly fed.

Suzanne Ondrus

I'm here and
they're on the screen.

But that screen has a reality:
    The blood runs
    The urine leaks
    The children cry
    The husbands shun

And I'm here sitting
taking violence as education in,
as something to consume
asking what are we to do?

It's been over ten years,
almost a generation.
We are separated by
an ocean, but unified
by blood, and yet our
country forgets that,
doesn't count that fact.

Sisters, today I gave
you what I could-
my energy to listen
and tomorrow I give
you my prayers for peace,
my prayers for healing.

Small, Small

Small, small
is how my father died.

Not a big, big light
illuminating his path

towards death, but a thin
trailing off,

a shedding of parts,
a tapering,
a slow reduction
of what used to boom
and bound,
foully snap,
and fully crap.

It's funny how we die.
Some go
in the space of a month,
an hour,
and some over decades.

I wondered how long
it would take my father to die.
It's not that I wondered when,
it's that I wondered how,

how he began
to go numb,
was it a hot heart
that built up anger
and built up anger
till it could hold no more?

Or was it like a blanket
that had gotten worn,
its stitching and fibers
pulled apart,
its color lost,
till it was just tattered
and frayed?

Small, small
is how we all die,
whether it is booming
outwards towards death,
or shrinking
inwards from it.

By small, small
my father became dead,
not calling,
not writing,
and not smiling,
And he got big, big.

The food
was between us;
it brought
us together and
was a way of speaking.

Instead of questioning
or hugging,
second plates
were substitutes.

Fried wontons,
shrimp chips,
bowls of pudding,
and heaps of orange chicken
made
full,

full
and
big,
big;

made it appear
that life
was there,
there going in
and going in.

But really there was silence.

Slow,
slow
silence
choking
us.

Dreams With the Dead

Last night I saw you again.
I was fleeing,
in an empty bus
and had to drive it, had to make
it go, and I didn't know how.

You were there.
You pointed out the
clutch and the gear shaft.
The bus was empty, but you were there.

Fleeing. Driving powerful.
The big and the empty.

I woke happy for your presence,
rounded
with the empty space
of the bus's curved
metal roof
and felt quite full.

Lingual Diversity

We share the bench
at a neighborhood park
by the court house,
watch children play.

He says something, points
to a running, laughing boy,
probably his son,
about the same age
as my daughter,
also running and laughing.
I nod and smile.

I point toward my little girl,
say the same thing in English
he most likely said
in his language.
He nods and smiles.

Like our children's laughter
we require no translation.

*

You stir this soup as if each finger
is warmed by the breeze
though your eyes close when salt is added

–small stones could bring it to life
overflow with branches , berries, wings
shimmering and far away dissolve

into a sea that has no word
for sitting at a table, naked
waiting for you to turn on the light

wrap your arms around a bowl
that's empty, a night no longer sure
it's the rim you're holding on to

that's circling a man eating alone
who can't see, hears only the waves
becoming lips, colder and colder.

*

This thin sheet has no strength left
spread out as a bed
no longer interested in love

though the edge still folds in
taking hold a frayed promise
pulling it to safety word by word

–look around, what was saved is paper
shrinking into curls and hollows
has a face, a mouth –all in writing

has the silence, the forever
death listens for –what it hears
is the unfolding face up

the way moonlight
has never forgotten your fingers
are constantly unpacking paper

as the frail sound oars make
when bringing back a sea
that was not cared for :this note

all this time forgotten, in a box
half wood, half smoke
as if it once lit up the world.

Simon Perchik

*

And though this bottle is empty
it drifts on by as if the grass
puts its trust in the thirst

for sunlight and butterflies
–drop by drop you water this grave
till it smells from salt

then sent off, comes back
night after night as a wave
telling you where, what happened.

Life's Catwalk

We walk the long walk.
The world looks on,
judge and jury of style,
our stride, our demeanor.

How well do we carry ourselves
in the skin-tight clothing nature gave us?
Our outfits neither Gucci nor Prada,
are dictated by climate and culture,
are indispensable, not disposable.

We are clad in white, brown, black,
and shades in between.
Distinctive marks are highlighted or hidden.
A mole on chin or cheek, a sign of beauty.
Unsightly, a blotched body lacking melanin,
or draped in a white coat of Albinism.

Some colors are never in season
in blinded corners of the world.

We live, love, give life
sustain our path with will and wit
in sickness and health
in sanity and madness.

Our pigmentations and frames
designated by DNA,
we walk this long walk
in the eyes of the world.

Catch of the Day

They stand before us
like potential buyers
of freshly caught fish.

Defenders of their shores,
their eyes seek out their version of our story.
Will they pull our eyelids apart, check our teeth?

Our worthiness is tested with peppering questions.
Salty threats thrown at our wounds.

The masks we wear hide fragile emotions,
brittle under hammering words.

They might have walked in our shoes.
Their stories locked away
in memory's dungeon,
they have chosen not to see
the repetition of history.

The catch of the day at borders,
which asylum will we get?
Political or mental?
Will we be cast back into the sea
of uncertainty?

They Do Not Break

(for my Caribbean people devastated by Hurricanes Irma and Maria, 2017)

They had rummaged
through scattered belongings,
picked up rain-soaked photo albums
blown off shelves,
and bits of a shattered chest of drawers
that held Grandma's diabetes
and pressure medication
and memories—baby teeth in a matchbox,
locks of hair and a photo in a plastic sack
from the first barbershop haircut
that showed the man
the boy would become.

Roofless houses
stand like skeletons,
their crowns ripped off
by vengeful winds.

Scattered in the road—zinc sheets,
branches, leaves, shoes,
a shredding rattan chair....

A neighbor's belongings
lie in the alley
behind an abandoned house.

A grey sky threatens another downpour.
Can't it see they are drained
after Irmaria's* battering?

They will gather mind and body,
dig deep into marrow
to stay tiredness in its march,
so they do not break,
so others do not have to
pick up their pieces, too.

** Irmaria: name given to the two hurricanes which hit the Leeward Caribbean islands one behind the other in 2017.*

Pronouncement

For how long have you told me
I do not belong?
Each time I wince at your pronouncement –

Until one day you colonized my soul,
Your voice overtook mine,
Now mine makes the cruel announcement.

Dialogue

Patient to therapist:
“I am so full of hate.”
Therapist to patient:
“Whose hate are you filled with?”
Patient to therapist:
“Is that why I am hearing voices?”
Therapist to patient:
“Among all these voices,
Do you recognize yours?”
The patient erupted
In uncontrollable sobs.
The therapist waited,
Offered the company
Of silence as the patient wept.
Then, therapist to patient:
“I will help you get your voice back.”
Patient to therapist:
“So that’s what this is –
Voice lessons.”
Then, for the longest time,
They spoke no words
Between them, but shared
The voice of silence
In their midst.

Robin Talbert

Golden Voices

On the day before Thanksgiving
The children dash out of the school bus
Tumbling onto the playground
Between
Two tall apartment buildings

Warm sun a surprise
Azure sky
Shouting laughing squealing
Voices ring
Arms exuberant
Feet crunch leaves

Running jumping twirling
No purpose
No destination
Because they can
Because they can't not

Until a parent a sitter a sibling
Calls them inside for
Pupusas
Injera
Bulgogi
Samosas
Pizza
Frijoles and
Leftovers

Liberty Enlightening the World

Give me your tired, your poor,
Your huddled masses yearning to breathe free,
The wretched refuse of your teeming shore.
Send these, the homeless, tempest-tossed, to me:
I lift my lamp beside the golden door.

– Emma Lazurus

The Statue of Liberty has a steel frame
and her skin is copper two cent's worth thick.
She's based on a wealthy Parisian dame
and the verse commissioned for her is slick,
even for a West-sider with a rise-again name.

Now this hollow giantess is dandled by her feet
from the sky hooks of a F35 Lightning 2.
Her Greek style drapery drops like a sheet,
exposing pure naked alarm: 'What is she to do?'
Her lamp flares as she's engulfed in white heat.

body declined

body plan
body paint
body-building

heavenly body
body terrestrial
body forth

body of ocean
body of research
body of whale

body work
body text
body plan

body double
body tattoo
body beautiful

bodyguard
body blow
bodysnatcher

body shackles
body pain
body fluids

body politic
body language
body of settlement

body of evidence
body of men
body of resistance

body bomb
body parts
body bag

body
body
body

Fetches from Izmir

Proud Izmir, once Smyrna, laid claim to fame
as the home of Homer, and as for its name –
it's derived from the trade in aromatic mrryh.

The beauty of the Hellenistic city,
clustering on the low ground
and rising tier over tier on the hillside,
was frequently praised by the ancients
and is celebrated on its coins.

More recently Izmir lives by its seafront kordon
(promenade), which, especially around leafy Alsancak,
is as fetching and lively as any in the world.

And today, they're selling lifejackets instead
of bikinis and no longer want the world eyes'
to see the neon wares hung outside boutiques.
One trader puts out his hand to a photographer
in a gesture that says 'No, please stop!'

Latest reports claim there's some doubt
the lifejackets on sale here will be good enough
to support any body in deep water.

Acknowledgments:

Stanza 2 is a 'found stanza' excerpted from Wikipedia.org
Stanza 3 is from LonelyPlanet.com

Refuge

for Teresa Acevedo

Since January, sun can't stop shivering.
Hope shakes her head, refuses to step out the front door,
so we drive to San Javier Mission to clear our hearts with mesquite smoke,
the thousand melted roses of perfumed candle wax.

Exhausted, we retreat from daily psychoses tweeted,
the Commander in Chief's confused sleight of hand.
Who knows who set off today's bomb on the D.C. mall?
Diversion is the strategy of an administration staffed with lies.

We pull into the parking lot and time reverses its hungry grind
in the hands of O'odham women stretching tortillas and fry bread
to drop on hot tops of burn barrels, into boiling Crisco
attended by dogs, kids and laughter soft as sand they stand on.

In the cathedral, red archangels watch us dip fingers
in bowls of holy water, our urgent need to cool nerves scraped raw
by news of thousands of migrant children crammed into cages
with no soap
or a change of clothes. What devotion can save them?

The thousand flames of votives offer no solution
near San Francisco's efigy under his serene blue cloth, but
who can resist lifting three times his sacred head?
Since the election, mass on the reservation is always full.

Entering the capilla, we enter our own wounds, say
prayers for the dead, for the health of friends, for love to end
public lies so loud we've become deaf to every crisis cry.
We drink in the heat of candle wax that drives tourists out.

Under the burning scalp of desert sun, we head for
ramadas fashioned from ocotillo arms and the trunks of
mesquite, for
fry bread crisp with grease, a homemade tortilla so thin
you can see your fingers waving on the other side.

we sit on unshaded railroad ties with Indigenous families
breathing the sweet tincture of mesquite smoke. A young girl
leans her head on her grandma's tshirt sleeve. Heat waves
shimmer us, distorted as alternative facts spinning our lives.

I Don't Want

to hear tree skin crying in hot wind, desert summer
pyroclastic as a broken heart, our hearts
crying while whales beach, bloated on plastic bags
and acid ocean along the coast named Pacific
when breakers and rip tides are not serene
just misty anger, smash and dash, the kind of dash
you want to run, ahead of a future where the animals die,
all the animals you never got to see in the wild
burning,
        chocolate-eyed giraffes
                        or elephants
                        Siberian tiger
                                    snow leopards
and in Madagascar, sweet eyed lemurs eating moths at night
before a tsunami from glaciers melts the edges of the Ross Sea
orangutans with their wise monk eyes
cheetahs running with me on their power pad paws
and wolves
wolves wolves
their ancestor stomach-stabbing howls
running over broken asphalt
Suits don't cry for burning
palo verde skin, thick as green leather
or green sea turtles belly-up and rotting on white Gulf sand
or five feet of ice falling at the end of June
in Mexico
this is such crap and I can't stop it by crying
but sometimes it helps when I've stretched the skin
at the corners of my mouth in too many smiles
to hide from screens burning out my retinas
so I'll not see clearly the end of the anthropocene, the end
of grizzly growls, barred owl claws, the magnificent flipping
of spinner dolphins
in the Sargasso Sea, the end of birdsong
and tears.

Zheny! Zheny!

Grandma cries, come out of your kitchens, drop
your laundry, wipe your babies' eyes,
link elbows and march the assaulted streets.
Grandma Anna knew invasions in her skin, the blood price
of a tyrant's lies, the way assassination is
not just a matter of bullets, steals sons
and daughters from the most orderly house.

Zheny, Zheny, where is that no good husband of yours?
Czech women were never known to comply.
The wren of freedom flew a lifetime in Grandma's oceanic eyes.
Unpinned her chestnut-gone-to-gray braid fell to her waist
as she told how she escaped the slave tenement
in Philadelphia where she was locked with other girls,
how she ran midnight streets to sing and dance, refusing
all her life one dictator after another to raise independent kids.

This morning the President's lovely wife stands behind his shoulder
turned toward the cameras. It's her birthday, and he doesn't rise
from his oval office throne for any woman singing in the room,
his manicured fists anchoring his kingdom. Mediocre student
who refused to read, he is centered in this sea of women
teachers of the year.
I can almost hear my grandma roll her r's stretching
the syllables of outrageous across her tongue.

Zheny Zheny Zheny, kick this no good out of your house
before he burns it down!

Three Facets of Refugee Status

1) Broken Wings
Watching dreams
Consumed by the fireworks
Falling from the sky
And spirits dampened
By scorching heat
From winds of un-ending war
Parents assembled
In the darkness of night
To undertake the journey
Into the realm of unknown.

2) Promised Land
Boat would accept no more.
Teary-eyed wife's hand waved
Trying to console husband on the shore.
The end of the perilous journey
Narrated by a Sufi singer,
"On the Mediterranean coast
Two fish out of water
One was a baby stingray
Another a refugee mother
With her unborn daughter."

3) Welcome Home
Father victim of cross-fire on a street
While mother and the newly born daughter
Arrived at the gate of refugee camp
And assigned a shiny blue tent
With time that morphed into a home.
Sustained under a banner that read:
"Earth without Borders."

Patricia Jabbeh Wesley, Adviser
four poems

Belonging

A Song to Dreamers

There's an ominous feeling when you discover
that after so many years of belonging,
you no longer belong.

A tree knows that the leaves it carries on its arms
belong the way water belongs to its banks
the way fire holds heat
the way a woman carries her fetus
the way the fetus belongs.

But there's something about a world where
some can never belong,
a country that never quits picking
out those who used to own the land.

How they pick them out like the way my Mamma
used to sit and pick out from the white
grains of parboiled rice, the dark wild
black grains, the unformed, the ones, killed
by sun and rain and the cold dew,

how Mamma sat all day, cleaning out the dark,
brown grains away before the cooking process.

Today, hundreds of thousands of children
who swam through swamps and ocean,
who came in baskets, tossed on the ocean,
who, so infant, they only cooed
their way here, children, whose mothers
sent them to safety or what they thought was safety,
like the mother of Moses,

and now, the new world of dark hearts
is shipping them away,
back to a land they do not belong.

To belong is to belong is to belong, is to know
you belong. But there is something ominous
about waking up at dawn, rolling
under your comforter,
and knowing the way we know our hands
and our fingers, that you do not belong.

Today, a man whose family came
from somewhere, is asking those who used
to belong to not belong anymore.
You see rocks and you see mountains
and you see swamp and you see trees
and you see sand on the ocean
and you see ground,
and you know they belong.

Only the feet of those not belonging, the new
homeless, the ones who wake up day to day
and belonged yesterday, but today,
do not belong. Those whose belonging
to America depends on who
sits up in that big white house.
There is something sad about belonging
to no country. There is something racist
about being a racist because a racist sees color
the way God can never see color.

Patricia Jabbeh Wesley, Adviser

On September 11

A Memorial to the Unknown

On September 11, I always think of the homeless
and all those unknown, the forgotten, street people,
those who sit in alleyways, on the stairways,

those who belong to nobody, the forgotten we see
along street corners, their shabby coats unfolding
stories we're too busy to read, their eyes, sunken

and alone, the aloneness of our manufactured world,
enfolding them as they wait as if waiting for us
or for tomorrow or for a god under the shadows

of buildings so built of steel, we thought they were
invincible, those with no name, whose names will
never grace a stone or wall or the lips of a grieving

mother or child or wife, those who were forgotten
in the count, the beggars, too ashamed to be beggars
until that morning when the first plane flew into

the first tower, and looking up, the second also fell,
the homeless with his old coat torn at the sleeve, his
food in a small cart he tooted around a city so alive,

the city forgot him, and I wonder how Heaven
remembers such heroes, and even as they ascended
into the Heavens, I wonder if somehow, the rich

and the poor, the homeless, the unknown coffee boy
at the corner bar, the unknown child who fled home
away from family until family forgot he was still

alive, and I wonder if the rising dead held hands, poor,
rich, the beloved and the unloved, and all those who
shaped the world before the world shattered us all,

and how I wonder how it felt holding hands like us
in our common tragedy, the gone, and those whose
bodies were so crushed, but in death, they rose

and rose above their killing, the beloved father
and the motherless run-away child, the street walker,
the black, the white, and the yellow skin?
Since no matter who we are, dying is dying,
the common denominator since blood is blood
and grief is as deep as grief and all our tears flow

all the same, and the heart pounds like a heart
in grief and in pain, no matter who we say we are.
I wonder as we remember, if they remember us.

Patricia Jabbeh Wesley, Adviser

When I meet My Ancestors

When my ancestors come to greet me
at the outskirts of the other world,
I will be carrying in my hands, all the bags
of leaves the wind has brought me
from my neighbor's yard.

When I cross over the threshold into the other
world, my ancestors will wonder
what it is I am carrying.

When I greet my ancestors, I will tell them
how my life has been littered by falling
leaves, falling dreams, falling skies.
I will tell my Fathers about a journey
they did not know I would take.
It is not the leaves alone I will be carrying.
It is not the heartache of living so far
away from home, I will be carrying.
It is not just the tears in a pail, I will be carrying.
It is not just the sore feet the wanderer carries
I will be bringing.

When I meet my Mothers, they will sit
me down on The Mat to wipe my eyes.
When I meet my Mothers, they will sit
me down on The Mat and wipe my eyes.
When I meet my mother,
she will sit me on her lap, and wipe my eyes.
When I meet my mother, she will sit
me on her lap and with her lappa,
she will wipe my eyes.
When I meet my mother, she will take
from my tired hands, this bundle of rotten
leaves and the pail of tears
I have brought to her.

When I meet my mother, she will sit

me in the middle of the room
just like she did when I came home
after years away at boarding school.
When I meet my mother,
she will sit me on her lap, and with her
lappa, she will dry my tears.

Patricia Jabbeh Wesley, Adviser

Tugbakeh

After Too Many Years

I was so long gone, when I finally arrived
in my hometown,
I could not find the road back home.

Time had swallowed up what used to be
the street into Mission Town, Tugbakeh,
down to my uncles' homes

where the fireplace was burning hot,
children hollering as night came in slowly
and the sun returned to its own home.

I could not find Ngalun, where we dipped
our pails and our feet at the same time
the way only villagers still do.

Today, I could not separate the mission
from the town or from the graveyard,
where the dead waited for God

to resurrect them on the day of resurrection,
on the day of our ancestral gods
meeting the other god, bestowed
upon us by the new-comers.

I did not find anyone I knew or who knew me.
I did not find the town I used to know,
and for a second, a woman thought
I was my Uncle Tugba's daughter,
and greeted me the way you greet
a wanderer from a far country.

She did not know me, and the man who
welcomed us out of roads that had become
only footpaths, and offered us seats,

and sat and sat as if this were not
my father's homeland, as if this were not
my father's homestead

When I finally saw my hometown, I had
become the lost daughter.
I had been so long gone, they did not
offer me kola nuts.

As if the town had run out of kola nuts
As if all the kola nut trees had been
burned in that same ugly war.

I had been so long gone, it was two days
before I realized the tragedy
of being denied kola nuts in my own town.

I forgot how abominable the sin of not
offering kola nut to a daughter on her
homecoming, how abominable

that empty greeting. I lost all sense
that the man in charge of our fathers'
homestead had forgotten

how to find kola nuts, how to slice
each half of the kola nut, how to wash
and place the sliced pieces

in the kola nut bowl, how to offer
the spiced pepper,
how to welcome home the daughter
who had been too long gone.

Light Verses Raining Napalm

for Phan Thi Kim Phúc

Splashing through puddles, you and I
The summer we both turned 9
If you could
If I could
Then we

But only
in subordination;
As if the subjects:
You and I
submitted to others'
clauses

Others' othering of
you in a foreign war

I: insubordinate
turned the page
to find you
naked
running toward the lens

I shouldn't have seen
You shouldn't have seen
puddle bombers, raining defoliants.
Wet and scorched, you ended
language, grammar, subordination
abolished diminutive endings
for little girls caught in the rain.

in the photo

I grin, eager to please
eager to be praised

my little blonde brother
picks his nose

my grandfather poses
an axe in one arm
a big headless turtle
in the other

after the photo
grandfather ruffles
my brother's hair and asks
if he's digging for gold

my brother cries for no reason
they call him a sensitive child

I am hero, finder of
the snap-jawed giant
beasts that eat
my grandfather's
ducks: the ducks
that he would have
eaten himself when
they fattened in the fall

it becomes a summer of headless
turtles, canned or frozen
preserving the taste of swamp
monsters for winter soup

Georgia Wilder

I enlarge the hole in a turtle
vertebra, wear it on a chain
I call it my turtlestone
beg forgiveness from
a bone locket that
never opens

today, I would put it on a black ribbon
choker to recall the guillotines:
one type of violence always
replacing the others.

A Noble Djinn

He was sitting on a stool in a corner of the square, or what passed for a square in the confined chaos of the medina. The late morning sun shone over walls of mud brick onto a face that was dignified, almost learned, and he smiled in a benign way at the hum of activity around him, vendors hawking their goods, tourists shuffling through vendor stalls cameras on the ready for every photo opportunity, and ordinary men, women and children making their way through the congestion of the souk.

"As-Salaam-Alaikum," he said as I approached, a traditional greeting that translates roughly as "peace be with you."

His complexion was light, lighter than that of the Arab population, but it had an almond tint that suggested mixed race. His hair was dark and curly, almost nappy, I thought, peppered with gray and his beard trimmed. His features were fine, his face thin, his nose long, and his mouth expressive beneath a cultivated brow and strong cheek bones. He could have been Arab, sub-Saharan, or Berber, or all three for all I knew, and since the peoples that had settled northern Africa were of Eurasian descent, it was the kind of face I could have found in almost any community around the Mediterranean.

"Alaikum-As-Salaam," I replied, the formulaic response that sounds so much better than the ubiquitous "you too," even in my tortured Arabic.

We were lost, my wife and I. Not desperately lost, mind you. Not call out the French Foreign Legion lost by any stretch of the imagination. Marrakech is not Fes, after all, where a wrong turn among its warren of alleyways, all nine thousand of them if you believe the local guides, can land you smack in the middle of the eighth century. But lost enough in what I'd come to regard as the raw energy of Marrakech to feel a twinge of panic, particularly with the heat of mid-day approaching, and I thought I'd use the time while my wife was browsing the stall of one of the vendors to take directions back to our riad.

"How does one get to the Jaama el Fna from here?" I asked.

It should have been a simple matter to make our way back. The old and venerable city of Marrakech had grown organically since its foundation over a thousand years ago in a hub and spoke pattern. All we had to do was find one of the spokes that ran inward toward the hub, the great square at the center of the medina known for centuries as the Jaama el Fna, Assemblage of the Dead, and, from there, the spoke that ran back out the other side to our accommodations near the Mellah, the quarter of the medina that used to house the city's Jews before they left Morocco after the last Great War for the Palestine.

But nothing about Morocco is ever simple, we'd learned, after almost the two weeks. In a country whose fables exist as a series of short stories nestled one within another over one thousand and one nights, it can be difficult to determine where one adventure ends and the next begins. Those mud and waddle walls might have been low enough to admit a little light upon our dilemma, but they were too high to block out any possible landmark that might have guided our way, the minaret of the Koutoubia mosque to the south and east, for example, or even the tops of the High Atlas Mountains to the south.

The old man signaled with a hand in the direction we'd been walking and explained in broken English that we should continue along that route to the first lane on the right, follow it until it ends, then left to the next intersection and right from there all the way to the square. His instructions were adequate, his delivery enchanting, and I felt myself taken with his kindness.

I dug into the pocket of my trousers and pulled out a two-dirham coin, about twenty-five cents on the exchange, but the man shook his head, as though I'd offended him. It had been one of the biggest dilemmas of our trip, deciding when to tip and how much. We were accustomed to the practice, of course – who isn't who calls their home the United States? – but there is always the risk of appearing condescending in that uniquely American way we have of making money the object of every encounter.

We'd been advised we couldn't photograph anyone in the medina, not without their consent, and often, we'd found after a couple of scenes in the medina of Fez I had little desire to repeat, not without remuneration. And then there was that little matter of Zakat, the Koranic tenet to give alms to the poor. Charity seemed the better part of discretion under the circumstances, even if there was the risk of getting it wrong.

"No want your money," he said, using the formal Arabic verb, subject, object sentence structure that suggested refinement. "Would ask a question instead."

I put the money back in my pocket and shrugged with embarrassment. A question? One silly little question? In exchange for directions to Jaama el Fna? No harm in a question, I thought, from a man who just spared me the trouble of wandering the narrow alleyways with no clue whatsoever where I was going, especially after I'd just made an ass of myself by offering him money.

I nodded.

"In Morocco you," the man asked, "why?"

We were strangers in his country, from a land that had turned belief in the Koran into a mortal sin, right up there with voicing opposition to the President's ban on Muslim immigrants from places he called "shit hole countries." Those are not sentiments I share, or at least I don't think I share them, but I suppose I twisted the prejudices of my own culture toward him into an act of hostility toward me. I'd struggled with the intensity of Marrakech after the staid atmosphere of Rabat and the cultured ambiance of Fes. I'd allowed every aggressive gesture, every grimace, every loud voice to take on a sinister motive since we'd arrived, and I suppose it was only natural to flinch with the question, especially when one is seeking directions to a square where the Sultans of old displayed the severed head of their enemies on pikes.

"Understand I would your motivation," he clarified. "Not your presence."

So, the old man just wanted to know why I'd chosen Morocco out of all of the marvelous places in the world we could have visited, and I had to chuckle with the way I'd projected my own ignorance onto him. Still, it was a question I don't ordinarily entertain – why? I'm content to do, not ruminate, and I figure most of my countrymen suffer from that same compulsion. I march my way through life with my eyes on the horizon. And I don't bother myself with existential questions, not when I'm from a country whose leaders pride themselves on their own "exceptionalism."

I'm an American, damn it. That's all anybody needs to know – or not.

And why, indeed, I had to ask myself. Why had we traveled to Morocco, my wife and I? Was it appropriate to share with the man the fact that my wife had decided she had to get me out of the rain of March back home before another bout of seasonally-affected depression set in? Or that her friend had booked the tour, and had asked if we wanted to come along? Or that we'd gotten a smoking deal on air fare, first class at the price of premium economy?

There had to be more to it than that, of that I was certain. Like Morocco is in Africa, for God's sake, the cradle of humanity. And there were the fables of romance and adventure, one thousand and one nights of them, of rich kingdoms, of powerful Sultans and beautiful princesses, of caravans, barbary pirates, djinns, and treasures of ancient wisdom. I'd read Edith Wharton's book, *On Morocco*, before we left, and I'd understood, or thought I had, when she described as "tantalizing" the utter romance of a caravan traversing what she called the barren landscape of red sand and stone in the distance. And there was Paul Bowles' kif-inspired book, *A Sheltering Sky*, of death and rebirth in which the female protagonist manages to reinvent herself in the Sahara.

As if Bogie and Ingrid Bergman weren't enough, or Jimmy Stewart and Doris Day, or John Malkovich and Debra Winger, or my personal favorites, Sean Connery and Candice Bergen, more for the story line of their movie, *The Wind and the Lion,* than Connery's dashing persona and Bergen's exquisite beauty. The Beatles made Marrakech one of their pilgrimages, as did Crosby, Stills, and Nash. I could still recite the lyrics of Nash's song from our collective youth, *Marrakesh Express*, after all these years, "Sweeping cobwebs from the edges of my mind/had to get away to see what we could find."

"Curiosity, I guess," I replied.

"Curious you, about Morocco?"

"I was," I said until I realized the response would sound arrogant. "I am."

"Had you expectations?"

The fact of the matter is, nothing about the country had been as I'd expected, beginning almost from the moment we'd landed in Casablanca. The airport was modern and efficient, with all the bells and whistles you find at any self-respecting international airport. The drive from Casablanca to our hotel in Rabat was dark, but the road itself was first class, smooth and well lit, a veritable interstate running north and east from Marrakech, or so the driver had informed me, all the way to Tangier. After a pleasant meal of tuna tartar and Moroccan salads with a more than passable bottle of Moroccan wine, we slept without difficulty in a room that could have passed for a competent four-star hotel in New York City. And in the morning, we awoke to a city that was clean and new, its boulevards wide, its public places white-washed and manicured.

"I don't know that I had any expectations," I replied.

There is no desert, I had learned, no barren landscape, not until we had crossed over the Middle Atlas Mountains. There are no fabled kingdoms, though evidence of their past is everywhere, and no djinns, not that I would recognize a djinn unless it popped out of a lantern looking like Barbara Eden. The land from the border with Algeria west to Tangier and then along the coast to Casablanca and inland to Fes and Marrakech is lush and fertile. The Atlas Mountains are taller and more imposing than I'd imagined, the High Atlas as rugged as the High Sierra, and the Sahara on the other side more desolate than Death Valley. The kasbahs of ancient sultanates still exist, but only as so many piles of rubble. The barbary pirates had been subdued by the Portuguese, the Spanish, and the French over a century ago, and if there are still caravans from Tangier to Timbuctoo, I'm certain their passage would be a desperate affair, an exercise in life and death, not adventure.

"Learn you did?"

The old man's questions were starting to feel a little tedious. What I'd learned or hadn't learned is a personal matter, not open to discussion with complete strangers. I consider myself a modern, sophisticated citizen of the world, a seasoned traveler – not easily impressed, and I don't relish sharing the vulnerability I worked so hard to conceal all my life with anybody but my wife, and then only on rare days.

"Yes, I learned," I said, "though I'm not sure what."

The old man shifted his position on his stool, turning his entire body toward me, opening himself up with his posture, and if anything, his smile deepened, from erudite to curious.

"Think hard you must."

The truth was nothing in my life to that point had prepared me for the beauty of Morocco. My senses were on continuous overload from the sights, sounds, and smells of the culture, from the aroma of tagines of chicken, beef, and lamb slow cooking over open flames, the colors and varieties of local fruits and vegetables and the mountains of spices on sale in the markets, and the chatter of women in their colorful kaftans and men in their djellabas going about their daily routines to the haunting melodies of the call to prayer. To say nothing of the bark of water sellers, snake charmers, fire breathers, dancers, acrobats, musicians and story tellers, and vendors moving their wares through the souks on donkeys and push carts to the shout, "balak, balak," move out of the way or get run over.

And I was run over as it turned out, on our first full day in the country, though not in the literal sense and not by any mere donkey or push cart.

It happened as we were exploring the gardens of Chellah, the site of a thirteenth century Marinid citadel built on a bluff overlooking the river Bou Regreg. The sweet fragrance of a blossom cracked my facade of studied indifference as we descended cobbled steps down to the mosque, minaret, madrassa, and necropolis at the lower end of the fortress, its invigorating scent penetrating slowly, inevitably into my consciousness. I awakened as from a dream to the mating call of storks, a vaguely Jurassic sound like the rattle of dried bones and the cackle of a crone feeding on fresh water eels in a spring-fed basin until I found myself standing in the derelict mosque.

I'm told the first word in the Koran is "knowledge," or some variant thereof, and that experience at Chellah was the beginning of my education. There are mysteries in the sensations of this world that transcend reason. That insight took hold beneath the scalloped archways and fluted columns like the wild blossom I saw growing from a mosaic above the archway between the mosque and the madrassa, its petals yellow against the red of the mud-brick and blue and green of the tiles. The seed had been planted, too fragile still to know whether it would thrive in the fallow clay of my own cynicism.

"It has to be the people," I said.

Our journey had carried us from Rabat east across the coastal plain to Fes, then south through the ante-Atlas, Middle Atlas, and High Atlas Mountains to Mergouza and the Sahara Desert, and from there west along the several hundred kilometers of the Road of One Thousand Kasbahs to Ouarzazate before leading us north again over the High Atlas Mountains finally to Marrakech. The landscape, lush and fertile between Rabat and Fes, turned barren through the mountains and desolate in the desert. At one point in the high desert valleys between the Middle Atlas and High Atlas Mountains, layers of ancient sediment penetrated the hardpack, a reminder that the land that would become Morocco once lay at the bottom of a vast inland sea, the very heart of a global land mass before enormous tectonic forces contrived to separate the continents. It was into this world of formidable deserts, towering mountains, and fertile plains that those first hominids of the species we would one day call homo sapiens wandered three hundred thousand years earlier.

The people who would form the backbone of the modern state of Morocco, a collection of tribes who identify themselves "Berber," have occupied the region for the better part of two hundred centuries. They built a culture over thousands of years across the breadth of north Africa that could withstand the encroachment of the ancient Egyptians, the Phoenicians, the Greeks, the Carthaginians, and the Romans, and closer to our time the Ottomans, the Portuguese, the Spanish, and the French through a form of passive aggression, appearing to assimilate while holding onto their distinctive culture as successive empires dashed themselves against the buttress of the High Atlas Mountains and the desolation of the Sahara Desert.

"Learned of the people?" the old man asked.

I'd been carrying around an impression of the people from the moment I'd boarded the Royal Air Maroc flight from Amsterdam to Casablanca. The flight crew wore the same uniforms one would expect to see on an international flight, parade-style for the men, military in every respect right down to the barred cuffs and epaulets on the shoulders, and business suits for the women, cut so close to their figures I wondered how they managed to breathe. They issued the same greetings I was accustomed to hearing, allowing of course for vagaries of translation. They went through the same pre-flight safety briefing before we launched and delivered the same in-flight service.

Everything about the flight, quite literally everything, was the same, except that it wasn't. I noticed an unsettling absence of formality among the flight crew, the usual spit and polish of carriers in the United States that can get you booted from a jet these days if you're not wary. I wasn't worried about the safety or security of our flight. That much was given, but I couldn't get over the impression that our flight crew was going through the motions. It was like they couldn't be bothered with protocol except for the expectations of the passengers, and I detected a certain amusement with our need for protocol beneath their carefully orchestrated charade.

"I learned of Moroccan people," I said. "Or perhaps it's more accurate to say I learned from them."

A few days after my experience in the Chellah, we found ourselves in an encampment of semi-nomads on the road south of Rabat through the Middle Atlas Mountains. The men were tending their flocks, but the women, two of them, invited us into one of their tents. The interior was lit by a single incandescent light bulb hung from the mast pole and powered, we were told, by a small solar panel mounted on the southern exposure of the tent. A wood fire burned in a makeshift oven constructed of cinderblock and a repurposed automobile grill serving as the cooking element. Rugs hung on the walls and laid over the ground kept the room bright and comfortable, if not outright cozy.

We couldn't have been more different, the members of our little group and our hosts. We were the intrepid westerners, my companions and I, the modern equivalent of those Victorian-era crusaders taking a paternal – read colonial – interest in the aboriginals, and these women were too busy with the responsibilities the season had thrust upon them to pay us much attention. And, still, I couldn't recall a single instant when either of them bristled with impatience or rejected our questions – how old are you, do your kids go to school, are you Amazon Prime members, and how do you manage without a Starbucks around the corner – as naïve and intrusive as they might have been. If anything, they seemed to regard us with a sort of good-natured indulgence, as though they couldn't fathom these busy people willing to venture forth from their tour bus to ask their busy little questions.

My interest piqued when one of the women, the younger one of the two, explained the circumstances of her marriage. Her husband, she told us, used to drive goats each summer through her village, a place she informed us was a seven day walk south and east from where we found them. This went on for years as the young woman grew from childhood to adolescence, never once speaking with the man who would become her husband-to-be. Then, one summer, the man showed up at their home to ask her father for her hand in marriage.

I never did learn to my satisfaction whether arranged marriage is still practiced in Morocco. I suspect in some parts of the country it is, and even where it isn't, I was assured that, in Morocco, the father takes a primary role in selection of a husband for his daughters. Any father, no matter his ethnicity, would want his precious little girl married to a man who can take care of her, and he's not going to give her up to a young man he has reason to believe can or will not. Except in Morocco, the daughter has little choice if her father refuses the offer of marriage, or accepts it for that matter, but to go along.

This woman was lovely, the kind you might expect to see in the board room of any Fortune 500 company, but for the matter of her dress, a head scarf and layers of brightly colored clothing selected, I was certain, for their insulating properties. She appeared strong and healthy, with attractive features and a clear complexion to go with a native intelligence that radiated from her hazel eyes. As the father of a daughter about her age, I couldn't help putting myself in her father's shoes. How could any man give this young woman away to a goat herder who would keep her in a tent a seven day walk from home, I had to ask myself, even if he does have a light bulb in his tent powered by a solar panel? But give her away he did, obviously, pleased I suppose with his choice, especially when the grandchildren I saw clinging to his daughter's legs started to arrive.

"They all seem so happy."

I don't know that happy was exactly the emotion I'd detected. Contented might have been a better description, but that wasn't entirely accurate either. Their lives are just so bloody difficult. But it wasn't resignation either.

I should have walked away right then, but I could see that my wife was concluding the transaction she'd been negotiating with the vendor, and the old man seemed to be driving at a question that had been bothering me for the past several days, since that moment in the Chellah. Something like what is it I seem to be missing from my white-bread American existence?

"Not happy, the people of your country?" he asked.

What could I say about the people of my own country? Happy doesn't describe us, nor does contented. Angry, perhaps. Afraid, almost certainly. Driven is more like it. Driven to cling to the baubles we possess and to acquire the baubles we don't, especially when somebody we know has managed to possess them.

All I could do was shrug.

"Islam," the old man prompted me. The word was uttered as a statement, but I understood it as a question. As in, have you considered the therapeutic value of Islam or something like that?

I knew just enough about Islam to be dangerous. It is one of the three great monotheistic religions, along with Christianity and Judaism, to trace their origin back to Abraham. And in their common origin, there seemed from my limited understanding to be more to connect than divide them.

Granted, Muslims don't believe that Jesus is the son of God, but that doesn't seem sufficient to justify antagonism if you're Christian. Jews don't believe Jesus is the Messiah, either, and Christians seem to think of Jews as God's chosen people. Muslims accept Jesus as a prophet, right up there with Adam, Noah and Abraham and a handful of other Biblical figures, and that's a hell of a lot better than the way Jews regard Jesus or Christians regard the Prophet Mohammed for that matter. The differences are artificial at best, more a matter of practice than substance. All three emphasize works and surrender to the will of God as the hallmarks of a righteous life, even if Christians in my circle have given up the emphasis on works for an obsession on the act of love and who is doing it and the Protestant work ethic has supplanted the will of God with the invisible hand of commerce.

I am prepared to believe that Islam is the only monotheistic religion committed to the well-being of its adherents, not just some foggy notion of salvation in some promised afterlife for the souls of people who toe the line in this life. The Prophet Mohammed may very well have stumbled upon the roots of happiness, or authentic well-being as positive psychologists of our day have taken to calling it, with his emphasis on generosity, gratitude, and a regimen of daily prayer together with the brutal discipline of Ramadan.

"Perhaps," I said.

And still there was something to the old man's question. His interest in me was a testament to the fact. Where in the world I inhabit would anyone attach so much importance to the motivations, expectations, and observations of a man he had only just met, quite literally, on the streets?

"Explain," the old man replied.

I was more inclined to look for reasons other than religion, and there were so many from which to choose. Like a sense of place, for example, something to which no American who is not indigenous can understand. A culture that has existed for thousands of years through the ups and downs of civilization. Monuments to the past littering the landscape that remind you that prosperity is transient. An emphasis on family, one generation to the next, that makes the investment in place and culture personal. Or an economy driven in large part by subsistence, and a way of life so difficult that it makes pining for things you don't possess an extravagance.

I have traveled in other lands that can lay claim to the same unnerving hospitality, Greece, Sicily and Turkey, in particular. And, as coincidence would have it, all of them have had experience with Islam – for better or worse depending upon whom you ask. All have been blessed with a strong sense of place, cultures that have thrived for thousands of years through periodic invasions, inspiring monuments to the past, and landscapes so harsh that personal ambition can feel at times like an indulgence.

"I can't," I confessed.

The most I was prepared to say is there is little reason to worry about what you have or don't have when life is so uncertain, particularly when you believe that everything, literally everything, is subject to the will of an implacable God. The generosity of the people and their sincere acceptance of strangers in their midst seemed enough to make up the difference. That and sensuality, that combination of delights that can captivate a man born in the heartland of America and raised on the spiritual equivalent of Wonder Bread with the potential of the senses. A religion that enables such beauty is deserving of respect.

"Remain you will, lost."

At that instant, I felt my wife's hand upon my shoulder.

"Did somebody say something about lost?" she asked as she stepped up beside me.

"This gentleman here is helping me with directions to the Jaama el Fna," I replied.

She smiled at the old man, and it was one of those smiles only a woman can offer, full of nurture and compassion and respect all wrapped up in one lovely expression of gratitude.

The old man placed a hand over his heart and nodded. "A most precious gift, lady, your smile."

I thanked the man and gathered my wife to make our way back.

"It's odd," I told her as we turned, "to think I had to come all the way to Morocco to find myself lost."

"But you do know how to get back, right?" my wife asked.

The old man chuckled behind us.

"In sha Allah," I heard him say, if God wills it.

Just Like That

Nick's wife, Afsanah, was a nurse and had the day off, so they decided to go for a picnic with their four-year-old daughter, Laya. It was a Wednesday, and the small park along the bay they went to was practically empty. Nick pushed Laya on the playground swings while Afsanah spread a combination of Iranian and American food across a blanket on the grass nearby. Then they sat in the shade of a tall eucalyptus tree and ate, watching the boats on the bay and the occasional passerby on the walkway.

An old man passed them walking a dog with brilliant white, bushy fur as Afsanah was putting things away in the basket after they'd finished. The dog stopped to sniff at them, and Laya knelt up and reached her hand out tentatively to touch its side.

"Go ahead," the old man told her. "He won't hurt you. He's very gentle."

Laya stood and moved her hand more boldly, scratching the dog between his ears. As she did, the dog turned his head and licked her hand. Laya looked up suddenly at the old man. He smiled down at her, then at Nick and Afsanah; they returned the same. The dog stood perfectly still as Laya moved her hand through the thick fur along his back.

"He's beautiful," Afsanah said.

The old man nodded with satisfaction. "He's a show dog. We just got back from a regional competition. He won third place."

"Wow," Nick said. "How about that, Laya?"

She grinned and nodded.

"Well," the old man said, "we'd better be on our way."

Laya stepped back, and they watched the pair move off down the walkway. The old man was short and dressed all in white: white tennis shoes, white socks, white pants, and a white windbreaker zipped to the chin of a deeply tanned and wrinkled face. He shuffled slightly as he walked. They watched the dog tug him a little onto the grass, where the old man stepped into a depression surrounding a sprinkler head, turned his right ankle, gave a little yelp, and fell on his side.

Afsanah reached him first, kneeling beside him. He lay grimacing and reaching his hand towards the ankle he'd twisted. The dog licked once at his face.

"I'm a nurse," Afsanah told him. "Let me look at your ankle."

He watched her as she gently lifted his ankle onto her lap and felt around it. Nick and Laya had come over and stood a few feet away watching, too. The old man winced as her fingertips probed the outside of his foot. The swelling there was evident under the white sock.

"I'm afraid you've sprained it," Afsanah said. "Not badly. You don't need to go to a hospital or see a doctor, but you do have to ice and elevate it as quickly as possible. How did you get here?"

Through clenched teeth, he hissed, "Drove."

"Where's your car?

"Over there." The old man cocked his head towards the row of diagonal parking spaces across the grass at the curb. "The silver Caddy."

They all looked at the car he indicated, which was parked just a few spaces from their own.

"Do you live close by?'

He turned slightly and winced again. "Couple miles."

"All right," Afsanah said. "Well, you can't drive yourself with that ankle, so I'll bring you home in our car, and Nick can follow in yours. Nick, help me get him standing."

They did. The old man draped his arm around Afsanah's shoulder and she supported him as he limped gingerly across the grass. The dog walked by his side with the leash dangling behind him. Nick gathered their picnic things, and they hurried ahead. At their sedan, he opened the passenger side door for the old man and the back door behind it for the dog. He and Afsanah helped the old man into the seat. Before Nick closed the door, the old man reached into his pants' pocket and gave his keys to Nick. He looked back and forth between the two of them and said, "Thanks."

The dog hopped up into the back, whining a little, and Nick closed that door, too. Afsanah arranged Layla in her booster seat on the other side of the dog, climbed in behind the wheel, and backed away. Nick got into the old man's big car, set the picnic basket and folded blanket on top of a pile of papers on the passenger seat, and followed closely behind.

Afsaneh drove slowly so Nick wouldn't lose sight of her. They passed their own section of town with its apartment buildings and crowded bungalows and entered an older, established neighborhood of wide tree-lined streets and large estate-like homes. Afsaneh turned into a long driveway and stopped in front of two-story home with columns and a fountain near its double-doors. Nick pulled in beside her, and they both turned off their engines.

As Nick lifted the picnic basket and blanket, he upset some of the papers on the passenger seat that fell onto the floormat. He set the picnic items on the driveway next to his open door and reached for the papers; by the recent dates and notations at the bottom of each, he saw that they were all printouts from various Internet web sites. The headline of one had to do with the need to limit immigration to the U.S. from Middle Eastern countries. Another was about a southern state's legislation to hold U.S. sponsors of Middle Eastern immigrants liable for any crimes they committed. The last was an online petition in support of the travel ban to the U.S. for some largely Muslim nations; words were scrawled in uneven handwriting on top that said, "Find out how to sign this."

Nick's eyebrows knit and he blinked at the papers he held, a chill crawling over him. He thought of meeting Afsaneh early in college after she'd come from Iran on a student visa; she was a couple of years ahead of him in school. Nick watched her help the old man out of the car, and thought of the extra shifts she put in at the hospital so he could stay home with Laya and work on his master's thesis. He watched his daughter with her sandy-colored hair like his and his wife's dark complexion smiling and rubbing the dog's fur from her booster seat, and shook his head. The water from the fountain gurgled quietly. He replaced the papers where they'd been on the seat, shook his head again, got out of the car, and carried the picnic items over to the sedan.

Nick handed Afsaneh the old man's keys as they passed him and unfastened Laya from her booster seat. He lifted her out of the car and the dog came behind her. Nick put the picnic items on the seat where the dog had been and followed them himself.

When he entered the house, Afsaneh already had the old man lying on his back on a couch in his big living room and was arranging throw pillows under his injured ankle. She unlaced his shoe on that foot, removed it carefully, and went into the kitchen. The old man held the back of one hand over his eyes and groaned. Grass stains stood out on the knees of the white pants. The dog nosed at the old man, then curled up on the floor next to him. Laya settled herself in a chair at the antique desk in the corner, took a sheet of paper from the computer printer beneath it, lifted a marker from a cup, and began to draw, humming as she did. Nick remained just inside the doorway and surveyed the room with its ornate furnishings and large gold-framed mirror over the fireplace. When his eyes fell on the old man, he felt his stare harden and his jaw clench.

A few moments later, Afsaneh returned to the room with a bag of frozen corn and a dish towel. She knelt at the foot of the couch, fitted the bag around the injured ankle where the swelling was most pronounced, and tied the towel loosely around it.

"Leave that on your ankle for as long as you can," she told the old man, "and keep your foot elevated like that. There's another bag of vegetables in the freezer you can rotate to when this one thaws, but don't move any more than necessary, and keep your weight off that foot when you do."

The old man had removed his hand from over his

eyes. He nodded.

Afsaneh looked towards the darkened interior of the house and asked, "Is there anyone here to help you?"

The old man shook his head. "My wife is dead. We had no children."

"All right. Well, the sprain isn't too bad, so you should be okay in a day or two. Just limit your movements and keep the ice on and the foot elevated, even when you go to bed tonight."

"My bedroom is upstairs," he said. "But I'll sleep right here." He gestured with his hand. "Can you hand me those afghans?"

Afsaneh took the two afghans off the high-backed chairs next to the couch along with one of the throw pillows on them. She lifted the old man's head and arranged the pillow under it, then spread the afghans over him.

He fingered the fabric, looked at her, and said, "My wife made these."

"They're lovely."

He nodded.

"Do you want a glass of water or something before we go?"

"No, I'm fine. I'm grateful for your help. I'd still be lying there on that grass if it wasn't for you."

Nick thought about the papers in the old man's car. "Come on, Laya," he said. It came out hard. "We're leaving."

Afsaneh gave him a puzzled look as Laya hopped down from the chair and brought the paper she'd been drawing on over to the old man. She held it out to him and said, "Here, I made you a picture. It's you and your dog."

The old man took it from her and studied it, nodding, a small smile creasing his lips. He set it on his chest, looked at her, and said, "Thank you."

She bent down, rubbed the dog's fur, then took Afsaneh's hand.

"So, you'll do what I've told you?" Afsaneh asked.

"I will, yes."

"All right, then."

They turned and came toward Nick. The old man

didn't return his stare. But his wife glared at him as she and Laya passed him. He closed the door firmly behind them.

*

The three of them drove home in silence except for Laya's humming. They went into their ground floor apartment through the back door that led into the kitchen. Laya continued into the living room where Nick and Afsaneh heard the television turn on. They put away the picnic items in tandem without speaking until Afsaneh finally said, "What was that all about?"

Nick closed the refrigerator door, turned, and faced her. He pursed his lips looking at her.

"Well?" she said.

"He had anti-Muslim rhetoric in his car." Nick spoke slowly and as evenly as he could. "News articles about curbing Middle Eastern immigration here and a petition supporting the travel ban."

His wife's expression didn't change, but she folded her arms across her chest. A long moment passed. Finally, she said quietly, "I see." She opened a cupboard and began placing picnic items in it. Nick watched the back of her. After another moment, she said, "That doesn't change the fact that he needed our help."

*

The next morning, Afsaneh rose early while Nick and Laya were still sleeping. She changed quietly into her nursing uniform and then busied herself in the kitchen. Nick silenced the alarm next to their bed when it woke him an hour or so later, dressed, and got Laya ready for preschool. When they came into the kitchen, Afsaneh had cereal, bowls, spoons, milk, glasses, and orange juice on the table. There was also an aroma of saffron in the air and a sealed Tupperware container on the counter.

"Good morning," Afsaneh said. They watched her gather her purse and pull on her jacket from a peg near the back door. "I have to catch my bus. Breakfast stuff is ready." She looked at Nick. "And I've made some Khoresh to heat up for dinner; it's in the fridge. There's also some in that container for the old man from yesterday. I want you to bring it to him after you drop Laya off at school and check on him. Ask him to show you his ankle and be sure the swelling has gone down. See if he needs anything."

Slowly, he shook his head. He said, "You can't be serious."

"I am." She leaned forward and kissed his cheek and then Laya's. She said, "Have a good day."

Nick was still shaking his head after the door closed behind her.

*

The old man's car was where he'd left it the day before when Nick came up the long driveway a little later. He parked in the same spot as the previous day, turned off the engine, and sat listening to it tick. He looked out across the manicured grounds, the stands of tall, well-maintained shrubs that separated the old man's property from his neighbors on both sides, the murmuring fountain. Hummingbirds hovered at a feeder dangling from one of the porch eaves. Nick blew out a breath, lifted the Tupperware container off the seat next to him, and walked to the front doors.

He heard shuffling from the living room inside after he rang the bell, and it took several minutes before one of the doors opened and the old man appeared in its cavity, the dog at his side. He was dressed exactly as he'd been the day before, but his clothes were rumpled and his hair was mussed. He looked as if he'd just awakened, but recognition soon filled his face. He dropped one hand on top of the dog's head and said, "Hello."

"My wife asked me to check on you," Nick said. "See if the swelling on your ankle has gone down."

The old man nodded and slowly extended the leg he'd injured. His pants slid up exposing the ankle; the swelling there was almost gone.

"See," the old man said. "Better. Thanks to your wife. And you."

"Mostly her."

The old man cocked his head and made a little shrug. Over his shoulder, Nick could see the tangle of afghans on the couch and the drawing Laya had made taped over the antique desk. It dangled alone there on the wall.

He extended the Tupperware container, still warm, and said, "This is for you, from my wife."

The old man frowned, then his eyes widened. He took it in both hands. "Smells wonderful."

"It's Koresh, an Iranian stew. It's good."

The old man looked from the container to Nick. Their eyes held. The old man said, "Please thank her for me."

"I will. Is there anything else you need?"

"No." He shook his head. "I'm fine."

Nick nodded and walked back to the driveway. When he passed the old man's car, he glanced in the passenger side window; there were no papers on the seat. He stopped, squinted, turned, and saw the old man watching him.

"There were papers on your passenger seat yesterday," Nick said. "Articles, those sorts of things. They're gone now."

"I threw them away," the old man said. "I don't want them anymore."

"Just like that."

"Yes." The old man paused. "Just like that."

They regarded each other while the dog whined quietly and nosed at the old man's leg. Nick turned towards the street and shook his head.

"Maybe your daughter can come over sometime to see my dog," the old man said. "Visit. Laya."

Nick looked back to him. He said, "I'll ask her."

Then he got in his car and backed out of the long driveway. As he turned onto the street, he looked back at the house. The old man was still standing in the open doorway; he raised one hand from the container he held and showed its palm. Nick did the same before driving away.

Sacrifice Paid Forward

There was a pounding on the front door. I lifted myself from the sofa and tiptoed to see who was there. Through the peek hole, I could see Ole Casey leaning against the door frame. I pulled the door open, and he stumbled in, collapsing half way across the threshold.

Casey writhed in pain, holding in what was left of his gut. His eyes bulged in fear. Across the hall, Miss Martha McCrea, his wife, leaned against her apartment door, her head bowed and bobbing. With one hand, she clutched her ten year old daughter, Jolie, who hid in the safety of her mother's shadow, dark red trickling down her legs. Martha's other hand clutched a rusted butcher's knife, blood dripping onto the threadbare carpet.

Miss Martha shivered and stuttered as she spoke. "You gonna save him, Dr. Edward?" Tears dripped from her chin. "Doc, you gonna save him?" She pleaded with terror-filled eyes, clutched little Jolie tighter, her knuckles white on the blade handle. I knew that if I answered yes, she'd finish the job.

I was down on one knee, my hand on Casey's neck. His pulse was weak, his breathing labored. A rhythmic gurgle came from his throat; he was drowning in his own blood.

Their near nightly screams and cries had permeated the building for years, Casey yelling and cursing in his drunken rages, his wife and daughter at his mercy. Theirs was a story destined to end tragically, a conclusion befitting the beast. We'd seen the bruises and black eyes, the hair pulled out in patches, the broken arm and fingers. I didn't have to think long. Right or wrong, I dragged Casey across my threshold.

"Don't worry yourself about that, Miss Martha. Some things are best left to God," I said. "Now go on, go inside. Tend to Jolie...wash everything down, and get rid of that knife."

She hesitated for a moment, nodded, and backed into her apartment, pulling Jolie in with her. When she latched their door, I closed mine and turned to Casey. Unable to move or speak, he lay on the linoleum floor, gurgling and bleeding out.

I wrestled with the possible consequences—with the Hippocratic oath I'd sworn to protect and preserve human life. What if preserving one life meant putting two others at risk? I was just a man surviving in a world where the fractured are cast aside, an urban sub-culture governed by animal instinct and common sense. Who was I to play God?

Casey's breathing was jagged and shallow. Blood pooled on the linoleum floor, foamed from the corners of his mouth. I turned away and opened the cabinet over the sink where I stored my bottles of courage. Both glasses were dirty in the sink. I rinsed one, no need for two. Casey had already had his last drink. Bottle in hand, I pulled a chair from the table and sat. I poured two fingers, threw them back, and repeated. I'd made my decision.

It took Casey an hour and fourteen minutes to succumb.

My flat was one room with a small kitchen in the corner. It was located on the second level of a three story walk up. Everyone on the floor shared the bathroom, shower, and the payphone at the end of the hall where we'd sit on the windowsill to talk. Often, just before daybreak, I'd sit there with my legs dangling over the fire escape, watching the sun rise with bright orange and red bursts of heaven—a new day to wash away the stench of yesterday.

We called the building The Bridge because it was like an extension between nowhere and the end—certainly the longest I've ever tried crossing. You can look out as far in the distance as you like and never glimpse the other side. Most folks, like myself, moved in at their lowest point after losing everything—thankful for a place to regain composure, though little hope of bouncing back. In my time here, few have left The Bridge on two feet. Just gotta keep your head up and never stop walking forward.

I threw back another finger or two and checked Casey's pulse once again—didn't need him coming to in the middle of an investigation. No sign of life. I opened the door and leaned over the railing, shouting down to the owner of the building on the first floor. "Miss Charlott, you up?" I yelled, repeatedly.

Miss Martha's door was ajar. She looked at me in question. I could tell she hadn't slept. Who could? I put my finger to my lips and motioned for her to go back inside, she complied as Charlott opened her door and yelled up at me, "Doc, what the hell is wrong with you? Its three fuckin' AM?!"

"I know" I replied, "Look, Casey got himself in a bit of trouble. I need you to call an ambulance and the cops."

"Why can't you do it?" she yelled back.

"I don't have any money, not even one thin dime. You have a house phone. Come on Miss Charlott, I think he's dying."

"Well save him, you're a doctor aren't you?"

Those words were like shards of glass in my brain. "Shit woman! Just call will ya?"

She slammed her door in a huff, ten minutes later the police arrived. "Upstairs," I heard Charlott say. Miss Martha cracked her door to peek out.

"Where's the injured person?" The detective asked, I pointed into my apartment. "There."

"What happened?" he asked, "I don't know, he banged on my door. When I opened up, he fell down. I dragged him in and did what I could. Then we called for an ambulance."

"Do you know him?" the detective asked.

"Sure," I replied, "He lives across the hall. I didn't knock on his door."

"Why not?" the detective demanded.

"Well, he has a little girl and a wife." I turned from Miss Martha's view and drew the officer closer. "His wife is a little slow, she doesn't properly understand things. Know what I mean?"

"So explain to me, why he would knock on your door instead of his own?"

"Probably because he knew I was a doctor...once."

The detective noticed the bottle and glass on the

table. "Looks like that was the second wrong choice he made tonight."

"What do you mean? I did everything I could do!"

"Yeah well, that's obvious." He replied, with a smirk.

The police took a number of pictures and questioned a few residents. They noticed Miss Martha, a woman of average stature, between forty-six and fifty years, worn and overworked, peeking through the crack of her door, but never spoke a word to her.

Once the authorities had completed their investigation, they packed their equipment and began the process of removal. Last to go was Casey's corpse, unceremoniously stuffed inside a black rubber body bag. I had somehow thought they'd wheel him out under a white sheet. The body bag was hard to see.

Miss Martha saw Casey being taken away and softly pounded her fist against the door frame. She lifted the front of her tattered dress and wiped her eyes with the hem. Jolie hugged her mother tighter and began to weep. Taking notice, in a sign of humanity rarely exhibited in this community, the lead detective approached Miss Martha for the first time and touched her shoulder. Jolie looked on from behind, a rag doll with yellow yarn hair hanging at her side.

The detective offered his condolences. "We'll see that he's taken care of, Ma'am. Don't you worry. It'll be fine."

Miss Martha nodded as the officials departed. Raising her head, our eyes met, and she mouthed the words, "Thank you, Jesus," and smiled through her tears.

I nodded, acknowledging the lifted burden, and wondered at what cost. Turning to enter my room, I caught a glimpse of little Jolie—her wide-eyed innocence, staring up at her mother's rarely seen smile.

*

Everyone who lived at The Bridge knew who Casey was, not to mention the dirty tricks and lowest deeds of humanity he'd performed to survive. He stood about five feet six inches tall with a basketball type belly mass, and dressed in all the latest neighborhood fashion trends, brightly colored and loud. It was the kind of clothing that people (black or white) living downtown wouldn't have found acceptable, but around here it was considered a status symbol, mostly because of the expense. That's how it's always been; if you had more than your neighbor, they looked up to you.

Had it not been for his association with the men who owned the corner bodega and local numbers racket, many a man would have taken him out. Fear of retribution was the only thing that kept him safe. Casey made a lot of money for those guys on the corner and, as long as the money flowed, they had his back. Now that he was gone, there were questions that needed answering.

Jackson "Crush" Ruiz was the ring leader of the Bodega crew. He was tall, young and very handsome, some even thought pretty. With his hair slicked back, pearl white teeth and manicured nails, he was a standout with the ladies. Rumor had it that he got his moniker because so many neighborhood ladies liked him. Truth be told, it had come years earlier when he took a sledge hammer to the skull of a former bully and rival who had disrespected him in public. From that point on, he was neighborhood royalty.

It didn't take long for Jackson "Crush" Ruiz to come knocking. Charlott was standing out front, showing off her new white-laced blouse. She usually held the post questioning everyone's comings and goings. When Ruiz and his crew approached, she stood defiant—didn't move or utter a word. As they entered the building and passed, she promptly entered her apartment and shut the door—the only two bedroom unit in the entire building, and with a separate bathroom.

The men walked halfway up the steps and stopped. Ruiz yelled, "Doc Ed!"

I didn't answer. No use in trying to be brave, I thought, they've come for me. I pulled the door open and made like everything was normal. It was anything but.

"Who's that calling my name?" There were two of them in the building and one out front.

"Well, I'll be damned," Ruiz said, laughing. "There is a doctor in the house." He had a big mischievous grin, his teeth gleaming like diamonds.

"What do you want?" I asked.

"You really don't want to play stupid, Doc. You know why I'm here. I want to know what happened to my boy."

"I don't really know. Seems he got into it with somebody who got the best of him. Then he comes knocking on my door. I tried, but there was nothing I could do."

"Well Doc, did he say anything, like who did it?"

"No, not a word. He could barely talk. He was holding his guts in with both hands. Nobody could talk in that condition."

"God damned!" Ruiz yelled, and pounded the banister.

His henchman said, "Boss, I need the toilet."

Ruiz turned angrily and snapped, "Well go! Do you need me to hold your fuckin' hand?"

I pointed to the bathroom.

"You sure he didn't say anything?"

"No, nothing," I replied.

"What about his ol' lady, you think she knows something?" At that point I knew I needed to come up with an excuse. Why not stick to the original? His next move would be to bang on her door. The henchman came out the bathroom. Ruiz looked him up and down. "I thought you needed to crap?" Walking down the steps the man turned and said, "I just as soon shit in the hall corner. I'll be out front." Ruiz shook his head and turned his attention back to me. "Well, what about her?"

"She's slow," I said. "Dumber than a sack of door knobs, and they got a ten-year-old girl that rivals her mother in intelligence. Sometimes you can't tell the mom from the kid. You'll get nothing there. No woman with half a mind would've put up with that piece of trash. You knew him."

Ruiz just listened as I spoke out of turn. I realized my mistake a little too late. "Look, I'm just saying, after he died, well you know how it is. People talk, and none of it's good. Most of it was about that little girl. Casey had devil problems. That's all I got to say on the matter, don't know what happened to your boy."

"Well sooner or later, the truth will rise and someone will fall. We'll talk again, Doc."

With that, he turned and walked down the steps. Charlott had come back out into the vestibule. She looked at Ruiz and rolled her eyes. He didn't take kindly to that and stopped. He asked, "That night of the killing, you hear anything Miss?"

"I got nothing to say to you or your thugs."

He smiled and grabbed a handful of her just treated Afro hair, yanking her head backward and forcing her against the wall. His knee was in the base of her spine. "I asked you a question."

Noticing the commotion, the two members of his crew ran back and stood in the doorway. I kept quiet and crouched down, watching through the banister.

"I'm sorry! I'm sorry!" cried Charlott, "I didn't see or hear anything, I swear, please..."

Ruiz let her go, wiping the oil of her hair on her new white blouse. "Good," he said, then yelled, "We'll be talking again real soon Doc, count on it!"

Crush Ruiz exited the building. Charlott was crying. When he was no longer within ear shot, she yelled, "Mother fucker! You mother fucker!" then entered her apartment and slammed the door.

I stood and turned to go back into my apartment. There in the corridor, standing halfway out of his room, was Chung, an aging immigrant American of Asian descent. Chung had moved into The Bridge three years earlier after being discharged from hospice. He'd been diagnosed with a terminal illness, and thought to have only months remaining. Unfortunately, Chung survived, not to mention outliving his medical insurance. He'd given away or donated all his worldly possessions, and was discharged virtually penniless, when he arrived at the Bridge. The possibility of Chung bouncing back wasn't an option; when he left it was going to be in a body bag.

"I hear everything, Doctor Edward, they no good scum of earth. Miss Charlott no call cops. I call cops. I not afraid."

"No Chung," I begged. "It's alright, we don't need any more trouble, they're gone. Let it be. Just let it be."

"If you say so, Doc Edward, you good man, I see what you do for lady apartment there." He pointed toward Martha's door.

"No Chung, I didn't do anything, hear me?" My heart jolted in my chest.

"You save her life, protect girl. He scum too, glad he gone. You do good, Doctor Edward."

"Ok, Chung, thank you. No cops. Our secret, ok?"

"Ok, you say so, Doc."

"I do Chung, I do ...thank you." Chung nodded his head and entered his room.

*

The months following Crush Ruiz's visit to The Bridge were tense. Even though there wasn't any solid evidence or proof of what transpired, Crush had his suspicions. His goons would come by periodically and harass the tenants. We all kept our guard up.

The Bridge experienced a steady flow of transients—many who weren't in it for the long haul, just a pit stop moving forward. That said, once in, you never knew how the dice would play out, one bad roll could make all the difference. Out of all, the most unlikely tenant stayed, the distinguished Dr. Ronald Clark. He was an unusual gentleman, well dressed and versed. He was in his late forties, carried himself with distinction and always wore the same outfit —plaid jacket, white shirt, black tie, shoes and slacks.

As time passed and it was evident that he wasn't leaving, the gossip started. Dr. Clark appeared very much out of place. Rumor had it that he taught school at one of those Ivy League colleges, which I assumed would make him a Phd, or something close. He didn't appear to be a drinker or druggie, just lost, like the rest of us.

According to the gospel of Miss Charlott, he was hiding out from the law. That being the case, she also let it be known that if anyone disturbed the Doc, they would be out on their butt. One really couldn't blame her, seeing as he paid six months rent in advance—especially since most of us were at least two months behind.

Eventually our paths did cross and I started referring to him as Dr. Ron. He lived in the room right above mine. The tenants on the third floor praised him. They said twice a week he'd get in the bathroom with a whole box of cleaning supplies and scrubbed until the place smelled as sanitary as a hospital. Myself, I just cleaned when I needed to use the facilities. Miss Charlott never paid anyone a decent dime to clean. Considering the load of crap, no pun intended, they had to deal with, most just abandoned the project half way through without notice, simply walked off the job. So it was always left up to the tenants, God knows Charlott wasn't about to get her hands dirty.

Prior to having met Dr. Ron formally, I would see him talking to Miss Martha in the stairwell. They departed the building around the same time in the morning. Martha had to drop Jolie off at school, the Doc just went off on his way. He appeared kind and respectful. I'd not seen Martha interact with a smile since Casey's demise. It seemed she withdrew from living, but little Jolie kept her from going over the edge. She got a part time job stocking shelves at the market about a half mile away. It did her good, gave her a sense of confidence and strength, and it showed. Dr. Ron took a shining to her, and seeing that did my heart a world of good.

As time passed, Chung's health began to deteriorate. Every day he'd set out on a walk, never making it any further than the front door and stoop. That's where he'd plant himself and chitchat with Miss Charlott. That, I must say, was a strange combination. The woman thumbed her nose at everyone, but took a genuine comfort in baring her soul and gossip to Chung who barely spoke English. Miss Martha developed a penchant for baking. On the weekends she and Jolie baked enough goods for the whole building. The smell alone was euphoric, the pastries and cakes she came up with, none of us could ever have afforded—well, maybe except the Doc. We'd spend fifty cents on a devil dog or ring-ding and called it a luxury. I asked her why she hadn't thought about selling some of her goods to help make ends meet. She said she had, but didn't sit well with the notion because she got all the ingredients for free—busted bags of flour and baking items that couldn't be sold were given to employees who wanted them. It gave her an activity she and Jolie could do together. Subconsciously, I imagined, it was also a way of paying it forward. After Casey, she strutted around with Jolie, proudly displaying heartfelt blessings.

There were times I wondered how I'd be viewed by God. For my part, there were many and continued sleepless nights, but I can't say I wouldn't repeat my actions. The situation restored a piece of me I thought was long gone, reconciling hard choices, doing the heart's bidding, taking charge and understanding the nature of humanity and the raw wealth of sacrifice.

The seasons changed rapidly, it seemed we raced through summer and barely had a chance to witness the harvest colors of autumn. The early frost and brisk winter's chill sent everyone into hibernation and seclusion. I got out as often as possible and walked in the blistering wind, leaves stirring and blowing like mini tornadoes—half colored and browning, frosted and dangling—waiting for their inevitable demise. Pumpkins and gourds froze on vegetable carts before their time. The cold of winter was upon us.

Chung, who made his daily pilgrimage to the stoop no matter what the weather, was always accompanied by Miss Charlott who found it in her heart to provide him with a much appreciated cup of tea, and wrapped a worn blanket around his shoulders. Like clockwork, Dr. Ron, Mrs. Martha and Jolie would run out of The Bridge in the early morning hours. We finally had a sense of normalcy and civility, and it felt good.

I got up every morning and sat on the hall windowsill next to the telephone. There was something about having coffee and watching the city come alive. The steady stream of delivery and garbage trucks throughout the boroughs, all weaving in and out of traffic, trying to stay ahead of one another. It was like a competition, whipping around corners, pausing at the pedestrian cross walk only if they had to. Most people just navigated the gauntlet and continued on their merry way, dangers notwithstanding. As I sat sipping coffee, all departing tenants waved and extended morning greetings. Despite the financial hardships and emotional circumstance the small blessings were quite apparent. Neither of us had any more than the other and we knew it. That bit of knowledge united us. We were all in this together.

Right before the Christmas holiday, Dr. Ron appeared to have taken up with what we used to refer to as a brick house —tall and curvy. She only made appearances late at night, coming in and going out. I'd overhear Doc's conversations from upstairs, barely audible, but you could definitely make out a woman's voice, and the annoying clicking of high heels prancing about the place. "Girl you look stunning, can't wait for you to spread those cheeks." Sayings like that were always followed by bursts of laughter, and then not too long after, I'd hear her leaving for the night. The heels made a distinctive sound, and curious, I'd crack my door just in time to see her shapely legs and behind as she went down the stairs.

I can't be certain, but I believe she was aware I watched from time to time. One evening she paused at the perfect spot, hoisted her skirt up high—way too high—to adjust her stockings. I let out a huge gulp and she chuckled, pulled down her skirt and journeyed on, giggling all the way out the door. This activity continued on for a while, the comings and goings.

Eventually it got the unwanted attention of Miss Charlott. She suspected something was askew. If it hadn't been for the fact that she thought an additional person was staying in Dr. Ron's room and there weren't any additional coins coming her way, it wouldn't have mattered. Two days before Christmas, late in the evening, Charlott was hanging a wreath in the hallway just beyond the vestibule, and in walks Brick House. She paused to remove her shoes so as not to make a noise, looked up before entering, and laid her heavily lashed and mascaraed eyes on Charlott.

Dumbfounded, Charlotte was unable to get a word

out—she just stared. Brick House does a complete about-face, whipped around with heels in hand, and beat it up the street in bare feet, disappearing into the night. That was the last we saw of the Brick House until New Year eve.

It was tradition at The Bridge for everyone to come into the halls just before midnight with whatever beverage they had or could afford—laughing and talking and wishing one another well. Chung was sitting in a chair in front of his room with a cone shaped birthday hat on his head. I pointed and laughed. He said, "No New Year for me, American Birthday!" The only person not present was Dr. Ron. Miss Charlott started counting down the seconds, "10-9-8-7-6-5-4-3-2-1," then she yelled, "Kiss my ass! Happy New Year!!"

Martha covered Jolie's ears, I yelled, "Charlott! We have a child up here."

"Oops! I'm sorry baby, I forgot myself," she replied, covering her mouth to conceal her Cheshire cat grin.

This was indeed a happy time. We finished our beverages and got a good laugh as Martha and Jolie banged pots and pans with a big spoon and paraded up and down the hall. Ten minutes or so passed and we said our good nights, each entering our own rooms, and closing behind us doors that protect, shield and keep hidden the strange and painful mysteries of our existence. There was a commonality of feeling grateful and blessed that we made it through another year.

Sometime before dawn there was a terrible racket. The doors of the vestibule were slammed back and forth against the walls. Then screaming cries and yells for help."Somebody help me, please!" Cries of horror filled the air, and every door in the building swung open. I raced down the stairs in time to see Brick House come flying in and land on the floor. She was screaming and crying, black mascara and ruby red lipstick smeared, stockings torn, blouse ripped. Her bright colored red wig in hand, crawling on all fours toward the nearest corner of the hall.

Jackson "Crush" Ruiz and his crew came bursting through the vestibule doors. The noise from the garbage trucks was so loud you could barely hear what they were shouting. "Fuckin faggot, queer bitch!" He yelled, all the while surrounding Brick House. Each of his crew took turns kicking and punching Brick House as she moaned and screamed and cried. I figured this to be my last day on earth, but it couldn't be allowed to continue.

"Leave her alone, you animals!" There was a blow to the side of my head and I went down.

Ruiz shouted, "What Doc? Now you decide to grow a pair, for a queer!" He pulled out a knife and turned to Brick House. "You want to be a bitch, let's make you one!"

As he lunged toward her, his goons grabbed her arms. Out of nowhere Chung came racing down the steps. Yelling inaudible words, he brandished a long samurai sword. "Yi Yi Yi Yi, Yi Yi Yi Yi!" Ruiz and his goons were stunned. They released Brick House and beat it for the door, nearly knocking one another over. Chung followed, and then we heard a loud thump and the screech of truck wheels. Miss Charlott helped me up and we went to the door. Jackson "Crush" Ruiz was lying under the wheels of a garbage truck, flat as a pizza. He couldn't have met a more fitting end. All of his crew scattered, not one stayed around out of loyalty.

I put my arms around Chung's fragile body, guided him back into the building, and sat him down on the steps. He looked up at me and whispered, "That's that." I patted his shoulder.

Miss Charlott helped Brick House to a sit up and pulled her torn blouse closed. "Doc, you better take a look at her," she said, giving me an all-knowing look. Brick House was obviously Dr. Ron in drag.

"You okay Miss? I'm a ... well used to be a doctor. Should we call an ambulance?"

"No, please don't; you'll do fine. Thank you." She lifted her wig and stretched it across her head, lopsided. "If you could just help me up the stairs... I was on my way to visit a friend. New Year's and all." She tried but failed to manage a smile through her tears. We all glanced around, no one let on that we knew the truth.

I hoisted Brick House up—her arm was around my shoulder and my arm was around her waist. Chung stood with a little difficulty and handed me his sword. "This would certainly have done the job," I said, with a chuckle. Chung smiled and grabbed the banister with both hands. We slowly made our way up the stairs. No one from the building opened a window or made a peep. We just wanted it to all go away, and it did. The police and ambulances stayed past daybreak. Ruiz was pronounced dead at the scene without fanfare—just gone.

A couple of days later, I was headed down the steps to the hall mail table. Dr. Ron came walking down behind me. When we reach the bottom, I said, "You missed some big excitement, New Year's Eve."

He bowed his head and adjusted the sunglasses on his face. Miss Charlott peeped in the hallway. "Yes I was told," he replied.

"I hope your friend is alright, she caught quite a beating."

"She's coming along." Doc paused, then reached up and removed his sunglasses, revealing a real shiner. "She's coming along just fine," he said. "Thank you, all."

He placed the glasses back on and headed out the door, leaning down to squeeze Chung's shoulder as he passed. Chung looked up without a clue.

Miss Charlott and I stood watching him go. "He doesn't know, does he?" I asked.

She smiled. "Probably not. Some things are best left in the dark." Brick House never made another appearance.

It was sometime in January that year when we lost Chung. He came out to sit on the stoop, as usual, and was greeted by Miss Charlott with a cup of tea. The snow was piled high; cars and trucks splashed slush halfway up the stairs as they whizzed by. Chung had been a bit on the quiet side that morning, just listening—which was fine with Miss Charlott. He stared up at a flock of geese flying over head, an unusual sight in the city, and pointed. "Going home," he said.

Miss Charlott looked up. "I think they're going south for the winter. They were probably too lazy to get an early start," she said, laughing. Chung smiled and released the cup. It shattered on the stoop. "Oh Chung," Miss Charlott exclaimed, "You broke the cup." She got up and went to gather the broken pieces. Chung's arm just dangled at his side. I was upstairs, perched on the windowsill. "Doc, you better get down here!" Charlott called.

When I got there, Charlott was on her knees amid the broken crockery. She was sobbing, holding Chung's hand. He was gone. I knelt down beside her, placed my hand on her shoulder and started picking up bits of the broken cup. Chung's eyes were open and he had a slight smile. He appeared comforted, which made me smile as I closed his eyes. Dr. Ron, Mrs. Martha and Jolie came bouncing down the stairs and off the stoop with morning greetings. None of them noticed Chung's demise. There would be an appropriate time to inform them later. Before notifying the authorities, Miss Charlott and I just sat there for a while with our friend and family member. I placed my arm around her shoulder and she continued to hold Chung's hand, and all was well. Chung, ahead of the rest of us, had finally crossed the bridge.

Robert Kostuck, Adviser

Black Sunday, 1935

Sunday, 7 April.

Weathered plank siding and clear panes of glass; coarse dirt drifted against the church's foundations. Wagons parked willy-nilly on all sides—I bring us to a stop and remove our Jenny from the harness and hitch her to a post. She nibbles coarse grass with three other mules and two dozen horses. Farmers, sharecroppers, families; everything gray and brown. Outside the door Reverend Mr. Lindahl spreads his arms. I step back two paces.

"Mrs. Bergstrom," he says. "You and the children will stay for dinner tonight? And before you protest, it's not in imposition."

"Mr. Lindahl," I say, "twelve miles at night on the River Road—"

"One imagines Kearney County, Kansas is one of the safest places in the world. Why, you'll be our guests. Alma's asked after you. She often goes on about your storytelling. It would do her a world of good to have another lady in the house to talk with. Nellie helps, of course; but she's only a girl. Alma needs another woman to boost her spirits. She's poorly. The doctor says it's the catarrh—all this dust makes it hard for her to breathe; sad to say, it gets worse with each passing day."

"I'm afraid the baby's coughing will disturb her."

"Alma loves children," he says. "Maybe there's something you need at Cott's General Store in Lakin? Beds for both you and the children. I'll send Daniel back to your farm to tell your husband."

"Thank you," I say. "We'll head into town directly after church."

His sermon touches on the parable of the loaves and

fishes, an intended message of hope. We have homes—shacks; chickens, cows, and mules—scrawny; crops—scanty. My neighbors and I tally future wagonloads of wheat; turn one egg into a dozen, a dozen eggs into a dozen dozen; and fill bushel baskets with apples and peaches. Foreclosures miraculously change to ownership titles free and clear. I admire and despise our small dreams.

Town doctors warn against the dust pneumonia. The land office says to rotate the crops every year. It has no advice for when there are no crops.

I will take what comes my way and be happy. Of despair I will have none.

*

"Nellie!" Mrs. Lindahl is shrill as an angry mouse. "Is everything ready? Sheets, quilts, washbasins, chamber pots, lamps filled with oil?"

"Yes, ma'am." Nellie's apron is threadbare and her blue calico hand-me-down skirt has an extender sewn inside the hem.

"Then continue your work in the kitchen." Nellie leaves the room. "My sister Clara's children—orphans. I'm trying to bring Nellie and Daniel up correctly—see this book? Dr. Cuthbertson's Guide to Raising Children. Because I've none of my own. And who's fault is that? Well, God had a say in making me barren. How old are they now?"

"Christina is seven, and Gunnar is six." I nod to my own children. They follow Nellie to the kitchen. "The baby is two months come next Sunday. We haven't named her yet."

"Of course I had no warning Einar was inviting guests—oh, Astrid, do sit down—I may call you Astrid, mayn't I? Dinner will be simple. We are plain folks." She rearranges the rug over her knees. "It must be wonderful living so close to the land. The newspaper men call it hardscrabble, a word harsh on the ear. With all these dry storms it must be quite a challenge."

"Carl hauls water by the bucket to the kitchen garden every day. It's all we've got. The prairie is reclaiming the fields. Oh, Mrs. Lindahl, if you could see those withered corn seedlings, and the wheat not even making an effort. Just plowed rows of baked soil. Then there's the Farm Relief Bill. We hope to—well—the government pays people not to grow crops—it's all about the price of wheat and corn. This Depression touches everyone and everything."

"Do you play contract bridge? I used to, until my health turned. I don't wish this life on anyone. Oh, yes, we had electricity brought in last year. One wonders how people have managed without it. I'd be lost without my reading lamp."

The simple dinner is roast chicken, mashed potatoes, green beans, carrots, dinner rolls, cheese, baked pears, and cherry pie.

After dinner I entertain everyone with some of the many folktales my mother taught me. I was sixteen when I emigrated from Sweden, and I remember everything that went before.

The bedsheets and chamber pots smell of lavender. Curtains billow and a motorcar chugs along the street. The clear sound of a piano and a woman's voice singing Beautiful Dreamer. I share the room with Christina and the baby; Gunnar has his own room.

I toss and turn on the feather bed.

*

Monday, 8 April.

"Daniel delivered the message?" Reverend Mr. Lindahl dismounts from his horse. Carl unhitches Jenny from our wagon.

"Yes, sir," says my husband. "Thank you for your hospitality to my family, and I hope your wife is feeling better."

"We've been blessed with a bit of a windfall this year—"

"I really don't—"

"This is not charity, Carl. It would only go to waste."

They unload sacks of rice, flour, and sugar; a mixed bushel of carrots, radishes, and onions; a cloth-covered crate of Nellie's pies, cakes, and cookies.

Excited to be home, the children chase a recently acquired puppy in circles.

We adults chat some more and when the Reverend realizes he will not be asked in, he mounts his horse and takes his leave. Carl strides to the well, hauls the buckets to the garden. The land around our house is dead—the big oak that was here before us is a skeleton.

"Charity," he says. "What else is it when it comes from a man wearing a dog collar?" He holds up a lettuce leaf pocked with holes. "Locusts, caterpillars, moths, even ants. "What the dust doesn't smother, the insects ravage. Tell me Astrid, why God does this to us. He demands so much and gives nothing in return."

"Now, more than ever, we have to believe."

"It gets worse with every passing season. There is no end to this weather."

"I shan't turn away."

In the house I sweep dust from the stove top and place a chunk of salt pork in a pan of beans soaked the night before. I tell Gunnar and Christina to bring in firewood. Every day they go farther afield and search the bare land and gravelly stream beds for fallen branches, sticks, even twigs. They've made it a game, counting footsteps until they find the overlooked chunk of timber or broken plank. I cover Nellie's crate with a piece of oilcloth and hang it and the sacks of staples from a crossbeam. I feed the stove with twists of prairie grass and shovel ashes out the door. The children return with bundles of wood, and Christina takes my place before the stove. Gunnar scatters feed for five chickens.

Carl's stiff back and shoulders, his sunburnt neck and brown arms. He scrapes shallow trenches next to each fledgling collard, lettuce, bush bean, snap pea, and potato plant. We want the water to soak deep, not pool on the surface. I follow him and cull withered leaves, shake dust from rosemary, thyme, mint, and lavender.

Another false sunset, a brownish-orange sky and the lingering heat of the day.

We wash hands and sit at the kitchen table.

"Come, Lord Jesus, be our Guest," says Carl, "and let Thy gifts to us be blessed. Amen."

Our meal is beans and salt bread, well water, and Nellie's pecan pie. Thinking I can't see, the children feed the puppy beans and pie from their spoons.

After supper Carl tunes his guitar and whole-heartedly launches into the favorites we always return to: *Hard Times, I Am a Poor Wayfaring Stranger, Life's Railway to Heaven, Speak to My Heart, The Spirit is Calling*. Even Gunnar and Christina know the words. Man and woman, boy and girl. Our voices float and weave across burnt stubble, thirsty stock, dried-up streams; across the thick night of the prairie.

"Mama, please sing the one about the river," says Christina.

"Why, that's a Sunday song," I say.

Carl is already strumming the chords. The vision has been on my mind. For five minutes I forget the twists and turns leading from a wedding ceremony to a sagging house, a sad Jenny in the stable, and one hundred and sixty acres of wind.

"Yes we'll gather at the river, the beautiful, the beautiful river;

Gather with the saints at the river, that flows by the throne of God."

When I'm finished prairie silence fills the room. The children quiver with an excitement I cannot pierce.

*

Wednesday, 10 April.

Carl fills four baskets with last year's squash and piles pieces of our old car on the wagon. Tire rims, steering wheel, two doors he's pried free, a sack of wires and spark plugs. He hitches up Jenny and guides her down the road. While he barters in Lakin the inescapable silence settles over the land. The wind refuses to stop and song sparrows huddle at the roof's edge.

I dip bread crusts in well water, apologize for my lack of milk. The baby sucks on the bread, turns away, and commences crying again. Too old to cry, Gunnar and Christina are struck dumb with sadness. The puppy has run away. They know about coyotes and hawks; they know hunger. That does not make it easier. Jenny nibbles handfuls of dried grass; we ration her hay. She flicks her tail and the flies swarm around her eyes. If an animal could speak what would she say?

The weather turns like a wheel—windy to calm and back again. Mornings and evenings are cloudless and tinted red and orange. Days are the blue-gray ash and high streaks of cloud that ripple and vanish.

The ones who came before built their homes from bricks of sod and the prairie cried out at her many wounds. At the far edge of our dead fields straight mounds of dirt mark the foundations of such a home. All we ever found were rusted tools, a broken bison skull, and scattered turquoise Indian beads. What people forget or abandon.

Carl returns just after noon. I wait until he's taken Jenny to the stable.

"I decided before I left that I wouldn't bring any of it back. A greengrocer and automobile repair garage took everything. Some of it for money—" and he sprinkles nickels, dimes, and quarters on the table—"and some in staples."

Vinegar, cooking oil, salt, coffee, and yet another sack of beans. Four bales of hay for Jenny, wax-paper wrapped sweets for the children.

*

Friday, 12 April.

Breakfast is salt bread and beans, the last of Nellie's sugar cookies. The well water tastes of iron. Early morning two heaped up Model Ts head west on the asphalt road. There are rumors of harvesting jobs, orchards of fruit and nuts, miles of cotton and onion fields. A green world of the imagination.

I boil soiled diapers in the big saucepan, then drape

them over a crumbling honeysuckle bush to dry. Overalls, linen shirts, a girl's dress, and everyone's undergarments.

"I imagine California," says Carl, "and it's all peach blossoms and grapefruit trees, but underneath is the same dry dirt. Better the enemy you know. This can't go on another year. It must turn to our advantage."

"The man from the bank—" I say.

"—can go to the devil. Another small loan for seed—who would say no? I'd rather eat steak and corn and drink milk every day—but I can't. That's a fact pure and simple."

A full day bringing water to delicate plants. We stand at the edge of what was supposed to be the wheat field.

"How can weeds live on air and sunlight?" I say.

"It's a cruel joke," he says. "Look. What do you see?"

"A horse and wagon—too far to know who it is. Drifts and dunes filling furrows."

"Look into the heat."

Rising heat—mirages—cool lakes, frog ponds, and rainbow waterfalls.

"Far away," I say, "so close."

After dinner we sing again. I feel empty, as people sometimes do when they pray without believing. The sound of the guitar sinks into the prairie night. Serious hearts for serious times.

My husband feels it too. He begins a new song we've heard on a radio several times when visiting neighbors, and looks right at me while singing about a paper moon over a cardboard sea.

*

A half-moon rises. I drape a damp sheet across the top of the baby's crib. Everyone in the house awake and waiting for the first of a hundred choking coughs of the night. Spitting thick air from dry mouths, shaking sheets and blankets, gulping water and never feeling cool or clean.

The baby stops crying in the night. I slide a twig into the stove's embers and light the lantern. She lies still in her tiny bed and stares at the underside of the roof and waves her fists in circles. I kneel by the bed and pray for rain.

*

Sunday, 14 April.

Fewer wagons and horses around the church.

"Where is everyone?" I say.

"Enjoying the cool weather on a day of rest?" says Carl. "We'll move the table outside in the shade of the house and eat our mid-day meal beneath the sky. Would you like that?"

The children smile—any little change a diversion.

"Mama," says Christina, "Gunnar crawled under the wagons and got all dirty."

"Tattling is a sin," I say to Christina. "And you, young man, what were you doing under the wagons?"

"Looking for our dog," says Gunnar.

"Well, then, that's all right. Angels don't always wear white gowns with gold trim. Sometimes they come in denim, broadcloth, or old flour sacks." I've sewn patches over patches and replaced missing buttons with safety pins.

Seated on the hard backless benches, we nod to neighbors we hardly see anymore.

"Isaiah chapter forty-one, verse ten," says Reverend Mr. Lindahl. "So do not fear, for I am with you; do not be dismayed, for I am your God. I will strengthen you and help you; I will uphold you with my righteous right hand."

What is strength, what is righteousness? What is starvation, ruination?

People cool themselves with paper fans that mimic the whisper of breezes through tall, green wheat. Am I the only one who knows what that means?

Arbor Day is two weeks away. Following the sermon Reverend Lindahl speaks on the importance of lay participation in building and maintaining the community.

"The twisters sweep away the topsoil and render the earth unproductive and unprofitable!" he says. "Is it any wonder banks foreclose and force us to act as tenant farmers on the land we once owned? Arbor Day is an opportunity for all of us to give back to the land that gave us birth, raised us up, the land where so many of us are buried and where the soil mixes with the blood. Trees slow the wind and keep Kansas from blowing away."

People smile. No one laughs.

"A member of this very congregation has kindly donated seedlings grown from the trees Charles Button planted on his return from the battlefields of Shiloh in 1871. Major Button would heartily approve of the further propagation of the seeds he planted sixty-four years ago."

Outside people accept small bundles of apple, plum, apricot, and cherry seedlings.

After the service I seek her out. Away from a bedridden guardian, Nellie reflects sunshine in her smile.

"I want to thank you again," I say. "We were touched by your kindness. I don't know when I've had the ingredients for a pie."

"The cherries were dry—I soaked them overnight and sometimes that's as good as fresh."

"I'd invite you to visit—we have little to offer."

"Mrs. Bergstrom, you have no idea how happy that makes me. Let's plan on a visit soon. Maybe next Sunday, if Aunt Alma approves? Daniel can take me on his horse—if that's all right with you—"

"You're both welcome. And you needn't bring anything."

"But I brought you this," she says.

A basket with more baked goods. A johnnycake, cookies, four loaves of brown bread and a dish of freshly churned butter.

I look around to see if Carl is watching, then cover the basket with a piece of burlap and place it in the back of our wagon.

"I can't repay your kindness," I say. "Simple as that."

"You repaid me by accepting my gift." Nellie looks at the thin crowd. "I only wish I could help everyone."

*

I place the butter dish and one of the loaves on the kitchen table. The children sprinkle sugar on their bread.

"Did I do the right thing?" I say.

"It would look foolish to return any of this now," says Carl.

We give thanks.

"It's beginning to feel like spring."

"The air smells different."

I throw off my apron and step outside. A long, low dark cloud stretches from north to east, and still no wind. As I watch the cloud gathers and rises, unhindered. Back in the kitchen we hurry to wrap the food in cloths and store everything in a steamer trunk. I hook the shutters and the children gather sheets. Carl brings in our mule's galvanized water tub and fills it with buckets from the well.

Gray and black, the dust storm reaches from one edge of the world to the other, taller than anything I could imagine. It swirls, roils, and punches fists against the bare earth.

We huddle on the floor. The wind pulls the window frame from the wall. Moving darkness flows into the house. The airborne soil covers the wet sheets covering us and turns to mud.

Time passes without measure. I become numb.

And when the day falls the stories fall with it.

And when the voice calls, we must answer.

The hand of God in everything we do or do not do.

The things that bind us may break apart or dissolve. The fading calls of the meadowlark and prairie chicken. Sodbusters who lost hope, hearth, and home.

*

Red streaks fill the darkness.

"It's letting up," says Carl.

He crawls out from under our dirt-covered tent. I grab his ankle. He shakes off my hand.

"Is this the end times?" says Christina. "Like Reverend Lindahl talked about?"

"Just another dust storm," I say. "Look. Starting to clear. I can see night instead of nothingness."

Carl returns with the lantern.

"The garden is buried in a foot of soil," he says. "Chickens are missing."

"Jenny."

"Busted out and gone. Must have been frightened something awful."

We shake out bedclothes and turn mattresses. Gunnar and Christina stare at me.

"We'll eat in the morning," I say.

The call of a passing owl in the lingering haze.

Heaven flickers with a thousand stars.

*

Monday, 15 April.

"Can't stop." Daniel reins in his horse on the River Road. "Everyone's going in all directions checking on neighbors. After I get to Kendall I'll turn around. Tell me what you need, I'll pass it on."

"We're done here," says Carl. "Tell the bank they can take back their land."

"He doesn't mean that." I shake a handful of silver coins. "Drinking water, firewood, and soap for washing up. And a doctor for the baby here. She's got the dust pneumonia."

His horse picks its way through soft drifted soil.

I pull up well water. After the dirt settles, I splash it over the children's hair and faces. Rinse and twist out a piece of cloth until their grins break through. I lie to them that Jenny will come back if we clean up her home. They rush across the farm yard to rake and sweep her stall. Their father sits on an overturned wheelbarrow and gazes at the sky.

"No charity," I say. "Those days are over." I start to wash his face and he stays my hand.

"God can't stand to look at the mess He's made. Draws a curtain over it all and forgets about us."

"Maybe the worst is past," I say. "Maybe this storm was the final blast, and after this—"

"I'm slow to anger, but right now I'm boiling." He

strides out to a pile of rocks at the edge of what was once a field and commences to throw stones at the sky.

I carry the baby's basket back to the house and cover it with a clean, wet sheet.

Gunnar and Christina refill the metal tub with water. We sweep and shovel dust. I wash every surface I can reach.

I scrape a thin, dirty layer from the butter and cut thick slices of bread.

Gunnar carries his bread and butter to the door and stares out. His father perches on the rock pile and slaps his dusty hat on his knee. The temperature rises.

Christina watches me nurse. The baby is more alert—a good sign.

"Mama," says my daughter, "I know it's not after-supper time, but—will you sing the river song?"

"Yes, mama," says my son. "Please?"

"Only if you sing with me," I say.

After a minute another voice joins in. Man and woman, boy and girl. Our voices float across the promised land.

Vicki Lindner, Adviser

Girls Hitchhike Across America

In Memory of Kathleen Stein, 1944-2011

There we were, really doing it, dark shades, pigtailed hair, self-conscious thumbs stuck out, me and my best friend, Kathy, slinging Army knapsacks jammed with sleeping bags, ponchos, a just-in-case dress, hitchhiking to California at last. Shedding the sticky drudgeries of Bard College, (black arm bands at graduation for the Vietnam War), desolate sex, the jobs we would soon have to get, lives guaranteed to march us into cheap Lower East Side apartments, hot flashes, and death, we swung up into tractor trailers that braked to loud, gasping halts ("Where You Girls Goin'?"), and made it to western Pennsylvania the first June night. That summer car radios blared a Motown hit, "Cool Jerk," and we boogied to its urgent piano downbeat on the highway shoulders of the great wide world:

Cool Jerk, Cool Jerk, Cool Jerk, Cool Jerk....

Come on, Baby...

Hitching across America was my idea. I don't know where or how I got it. I was reading *The Confessions of St. Augustine,* my hair falling out in clumps, not On the Road by Jack Kerouac. I'd been a sedentary virgin, more or less, until the previous spring when I'd slept with a poet who tilted his Bultaco 200 into the wind. He soon claimed he never loved me as we spun into Hudson Valley apple petals drifting toward the corrosive leaves of fall. So I grew thin, began nurturing an unrequited passion for an L.A. harmonica player. Kathy's bf had run off with a small-breasted frosh, so she was screwing a townie river rat, earning a D in "19th Century Literature: A Marxist Approach." We'd just been caught stuffing our purses with sugared almonds in a Red Hook supermarket, nice college girls, middle class, stealing, alas. Sprawled disconsolately on my dormitory bed, downing an amphetamine, an historic muse gripped me: Go West! "Let's hitchhike to California after graduation," I proposed, and Kathy, peering like Thisbe from her wall of black hair, bravely said, "Sure!"

This was a bad idea in 1966, a dangerous, screwball, pre-Hippie notion. We dared not tell her parents; mine were aghast. We would be Raped! Murdered! Shot! Killed! Knifed! *Whyyyyyy* not buy a little Volkswagen? Or take a Greyhound! Distracted by the rapturous high of busting out of safety's strait jacket, I recall nothing of my parents' pleading harangues. For once it seemed possible to be ecstatically fearless. In the end, my father, wryly disclaiming our anarchic plan, drove us to the edge of our first highway: New Jersey's Route 46. I did promise to call home every night, collect.

For long distance phone calls I could spare no coins. We had, I remember, three hundred dollars apiece to last three months. We had to wend cheaply. In Carlisle, Pennsylvania we wangled a room in a Dickinson College dormitory. After that, we thumbed to towns where we could freeload off relatives.

In Illinois was Kathy's second cousin, who twenty years before had shot her lover's boyfriend and gotten off because her father was a judge. We holed up in the murderess's gingerbread mansion, hulking in its enchanted forest of diseased elms.

In St. Louis we sponged off my mother's half-sister, married six times, once to a bigamist, now to a muttering curmudgeon, who scrawled dirty pictures and showed them to us.

We dropped in on my favorite aunt, white hair pleated with turquoise combs, screaming at her nasty pet raccoon in the Arizona desert, and her husband, a first mate she'd met on the ship sailing her home from a bad marriage in Italy, where she'd sung opera in her sweet coloratura for the last time. Undoing his pipe from his arthritic claws, Uncle Jim expectorated his vivid sailor's curses, inspired by the mad giggles of Kathy, loathed on sight by my cousin and especially the jealous girlfriend she'd brought home from the WACS.

In Dallas, an aunt we'd targeted for free hospitality, a salesperson at Neiman Marcus, saw our oil-stained ankles and filthy packs sullying her fur department and declined to harbor us.

Between dwellings tied to our blood, we bunked with old boyfriends, friends of friends, The Salvation Army, and in a five dollar Flagstaff flophouse, neon flashing on the soggy doughnut bed.

When there were no cheap or free digs we camped, shivering through lightning storms in the outhouse, or under picnic tables, rain-proofed with plastic. Strangers invited us to leave the ground beneath the thundering sky and shelter in their cozy tents. They wanted to be us, we bet. We flung our packs down into these occupied territories, shouldered them back up and floated out, leaving miscellaneous lives stuck in their secrets.

We reached Colorado in a speedy three weeks. In Silverton, the police arrested us for hitchhiking and put us on a train. From Boulder, we walked into Rocky Mountain National Park, where the astonished ranger at the toll booth let us in gratis. After that we thumbed South, and with most of the summer quivering before us, hopped a third class bus to Mexico City (three days passed out in the back), got shit-faced on Reforma margaritas, picked up a couple of suave dudes in Taxco, were pursued by mad dogs on Calle de Los Muertos, by mota, mosquitoes in San Blas, trained up to Guaymus, then to the California border. In L.A., Mecca!, waited the harmonica player, blond forelock floating onto flat cheeks as he sifted blues through his silver harp. We arrived at his tiny apartment with bad cases of diarrhea and stayed for five weeks, but he never loved me.

Give me a little bit of bass with those eighty-eights

Mmmmmmm Aahhhhhh Cookin'.....Smokin!

That Cool Jerk summer we led charmed lives. We were never raped and we didn't die. In retrospect, I'm not sure why: Our new self-images, carefully contrived, might have protected us like ju-ju pouches. We were girls on the lam, Peter Pans flying on a wire, propelled by invincible naiveté, and androgynous joy. We were not quite flesh and blood versions of ourselves, performing in our real lives' proscenium.

At the time, we believed ourselves in control of our liberated destinies and attributed our survival to the ingenious safety system we had devised. We never got in a car that had more than one man in it. When a rusted Fury braked to a fuming hiatus and the driver inquired, "Where you girls going?" we stuck out our chins and asked, "Where are you going?" We got in, provided he had a quick answer and was headed in our direction. If he hesitated, or was careening around the bend, we let him pass by. We never hitched at night. One of us sat in the front, the other in back, prepared to choke the chauffeur if he tried anything funny. We prided ourselves on being able to discern the moral character of any individual. We both carried whistles and four-inch sheathed knives. (When we revealed these weapons to the driver of the red Thunderbird that whizzed us all the way from Kansas City to Denver, he guffawed. "What would you do," he asked me, squashed in the boot, "if I held a gun to her head and drove off the highway?").

Small town America enabled our coo-coo sojourn by rescuing endangered female vagabonds from vicious criminals. Families, on their way to church, would drive miles out of their way to drop us at an on-ramp, lecturing us about foolhardiness, recounting the deaths of locals who'd been murdered, robbed, molested while hitchhiking. After we snapped their sedan doors shut we laughed.

The danger we did encounter passed through our consciousness like a late night movie on a flickering screen: The drunk lurching his Buick into reverse on a Texas highway; the mute black man who drove us to the wrong side of a river in Louisiana; the courteous truck driver, drawling that he had a motel room, three pairs of pajamas at the ready. Hot rods dragging mufflers passed us on Main Street, turned, smoked by again. We cherished the tension, which felt like great sex that hasn't happened yet, but might have been death, violation, a maniac's forbidden pleasure suppressed.

And we kept testing our ability to pass through Inferno's circles unharmed. In Los Angeles, not in bed with the harmonica player, we ran out of money. Kathy got a job with a detective that specialized in busting employees who stole from See's Candy cash registers. I signed on with a temporary agency and trudged off to type in a square and windowless fortress. Trapped in this metaphor for what I feared was my future, I felt unfairly stifled. So I quit, answered a suspicious ad in the Los Angeles Times: "Wanted: a secretary with a sense of honor to type, run errands for an elderly man suffering from a lengthy illness."

Ready for anything that wasn't boring, I took the bus to a West Hollywood apartment. The ad's author was Kali, a young, blond prostitute, known as "The Barefoot Contessa," until she did mucho jail time for selling kilos of grass. She was hooking to get her man, Lou, a fortyish jazz singer, off uppers —his "lengthy illness." Lou wasn't cooperating, gulped handfuls of "medicine" as I transported him to his very private doctor, lurching through red lights in a stick shift car I hadn't the slightest idea how to operate. When the Johns rang the buzzer, Kali hid her lover in the closet and turned up the music. I stayed busy at the Remington as Lou's recorded drone, "I'm in the moooood for love," cushioned the grunts and heavy breathing. In the ten days I worked for Kali, I typed up a suitcase full of cute aphorisms that the couple, inspired by Methedrine, had scribbled on scraps. ("What's so common about sense? Ain't much of it around town.") Then, stuffing them in envelopes, I submitted them to The Reader's Digest, a dozen at a time.

One afternoon when Kali was "peddling her ass," that is, riding her bicycle around Hollywood, drumming up customers, a John called for an appointment. I told him she was out with my usual line, "I- know- this- is- hard- to- believe- but- I- am- her- secretary, no- not- another- hooker." He sucked in his breath. "Hey, you're the kind of gal I want to be with!" he exclaimed and offered me a thousand dollars. For the first time in weeks, I saw myself as I really was– skinny, pimply, wearing a brown dress my mother had made, wild, frizzy hair pinned into a demure French twist– and saw fit to decline. My harmonica player was amazed: "A thousand a throw? Sight unseen?" Shit, he'd have done it for five hundred, maybe fifty! It was time to get back on Route 66, the unreal road.

At the on-ramp in Southern California, drivers bypassed male hitchhikers, waiting for days for a ride, to pick up us girls, as we headed for Texas, Louisiana, then home. In Florida we thumbed to the Greyhound station, so Kathy's parents could fantasize we'd arrived by bus. Our final driver, amazed to hear that we'd hitched about six thousand miles, let us out of his steaming truck at the door of my parent's suburban house, my childhood abode, to my altered consciousness no longer the place I had started out.

In 1966 I was not a writer. These sketchy scenes are all I remember about my hitchhiking trip. I did keep a journal the first few days, then stopped, as it wasn't easy to fish the rain-soaked notebook out of my knapsack, or write on jolting trucks in the dark. For those ephemeral three months, the best of my life, I was after pure experience, not a literary distillation of it. The memorabilia that survive consist of fifteen wallet-sized, black and white Instamatic photographs, some shadowed by a poisonous orange stain. These photos do little to fill memory's gaps; most seem to have been shot with a smirk, as if the photographer knew that the subject was a joke.

Here are two out-of-focus back views of Kathy, trundling her pack across a wooden bridge, and a blurry image of a winged monument, chopped off at the top; another shows her, face buried in her knees, warming her butt over a camp fire grate. The most revealing is a head and shoulders shot of me, with dark glasses and bandanna-bound head, assuming an irate expression I must have thought tough beneath a black and white sign: Pedestrians-Bicycles-Motor Scooters-Motorized Bicycles-Animals Led- Ridden- or-Driven–PROHIBITED!" I stuck my thumb out defiantly as the shutter clicked:

...them guys looking at me like I'm a fool

Deep Down Inside They Know I'm Cool...

I'm the King of the Cool Jerks.

And that is the spirit most worth remembering a few months before my seventieth birthday: Defying what girls were supposed to do, switching caution and common sense for androgynous, tough anger, and I'll- stick- out-my -thumb -if -I -feel- like –it- Fuck You, the have- to-dance rhythm instead of strings-attached sex. In the hot dust of an unknown town, barely seen but passed through, a woman friend becomes an extension of self, and a leg up on the fender floats us into the world's largest truck. We needed only our bodies to fly West, as should-do's fell out of our brains like cat hair while plastic whistles protected us from death.

This was a beginning—after that I never did what girls raised in the fifties were supposed to do—and also an end. By late fall, Kathy and I were residents of Loisada Manhattan apartments, with DC current and bathtubs in the kitchen, making ninety a week as editorial assistants for sleazy mags, True Confessions and Modern Romance. I had a Vidal Sassoon haircut, false lashes, and a heart wound in anxious coils over a married actor. Kathy talked a guy with a knife out of raping her on the stairs of her Eleventh Street tenement. Still, we planned to hitchhike wherever we went until death did us part.

On our final journey, a year later, we got a ride upstate with a weirdo who stopped at every small town pharmacy to fill his prescription for codeine cough syrup, chugged the bottles and shattered them out the window, SMASH, his eyes whirling pinwheel circles as he stomped the gas pedal to the floor so we couldn't jump out.

It was 1967, we were tax-paying women, and the Cool Jerk summer was part of the past.

"Girls Hitchhike" first appeared in *Grand Tour: The Journal of Travel Literature*, edited by Jason Wilson.

Photographs courtesy of the author.

The Obligation

> *Do not be daunted by the enormity of the world's grief. Do justly now. Love mercy now. Walk humbly now. You are not obligated to complete the work, but neither are you free to abandon it.*
> *~ The Talmud*

When we were children, our mother sometimes cooked up a pot of split pea soup for lunch. She flavored it with onions and ham hocks. The ham hocks not only tasted good with their pink saltiness, the sweetness of the fat, and the chewy, dimpled skin, they were packed with tiny squarish bones, which we cleaned with devotion until they shone slippery blue-white. It surprises me now, but our mother let us play with them, stacking them and lining them up on the table like houses along a street. In an unspoken understanding of the symbolism, we called the assemblage Jerome, the name of a ghost town we had visited in Arizona. Near the end of high school, in the mid-nineteen sixties, I would think of those rows of bones as a diorama of Rehoboth Mission, the hub of our church's many smaller missions in the Navajo Nation. It was the place where I spent most of my school years, sometimes as a boarding student, sometimes as a day student, always as the child of white missionaries. I envisioned a single knucklebone representing each house on the mission compound, a stack of bones as the institutional buildings—the hospital, the schools, the church. I had by then grown deeply critical of things I witnessed there, and I mentally connected the rows of knucklebones to Jesus' words: "Woe to you, teachers of the law ..., you hypocrites! You are like whitewashed tombs, which look beautiful on the outside but on the inside are full of the bones of the dead and everything unclean." That's how I felt about Rehoboth by the end of my schooling. The intensity of those feelings only grew as

I moved into adulthood.

More than fifty years after I graduated, I have lived oceans away from the mission, and yet, the mission is always with me. It continues to frequent my night dreams. In them, I usually find myself in the high school, always in the hallway. It is dark there, the walls lined with military green lockers. Sometimes I am missing essential clothing, sometimes trying to get to class, never making it. Other times I have no pencils, and that is of vital and frightening importance. Each time, the dream ends when at last I remember that I succeeded in graduating from high school long ago.

The majority of dream researchers and theorists agree that recurrent dreams call attention to unresolved problems in the life of the dreamer and that a powerful dream image may provide a context for an unsettling emotion or conflict. Whenever I return to the mission in real life, whether for a nephew's graduation party or a wedding or a funeral, I feel those unfinished conflicts in my stomach—the ones symbolized by that long, dark hallway. I relive memories of times long past. I think of my Navajo friends and stories they have told and continue to tell about their years at the mission. I remember my own years there. The dream that returns to me over and over tells me that there is something I have left undone. Maybe it is something that I, more than half a century after apparently having finished with Rehoboth, am still obligated to do.

So many questions arise out of the brokenness that I was a part of, the main one being "What is my responsibility regarding this tear in the fabric of the world?" Because I grew up in the Navajo Nation, I was the recipient of a wealth of experiences uncommon to most white people. I ask myself if I owe more than others because of this. "Have these experiences equipped me in a way that also obligates me?" And, "Just how do I extend myself in a way that is truly helpful and meaningful without appropriating a task that might not belong to me?" I have been afraid to reach out in a hand of reconciliation—afraid of doing it wrong, afraid of having any overture rejected, especially by people I care for. Afraid I will be misunderstood.

Fania Davis Jordan is a civil rights attorney and

executive director of Restorative Justice for Oakland Youth. She also happens to be the sister of Angela Davis. The murders of Michael Brown and Eric Garner and the subsequent decisions not to indict the police officers that killed them served as the immediate impetus for her July 2016 article in Yes Magazine, "This Country Needs a Truth and Reconciliation Process on Violence Against African Americans—Right Now." I know I am not alone in finding the thought of a national truth and reconciliation process overwhelming, although I believe it is absolutely needed. I can't help asking myself if my nighttime journeys to those darkened Rehoboth hallways continue to plague me because my share in the history of the mission constrains me in a particular way to be part of a reconciliation process within the Navajo Nation.

Rehoboth Mission got its start in 1903. My high school history teacher, a white former missionary kid like me, told us that the land for the mission was obtained through the Homestead Act. He said that two Dutch women, Miss Russbach and Miss Hartog, staked the claim. I imagined stern, intrepid women in long black dresses urging a team of horses from the seat of their buckboard wagon, dust swirling around them, leaping down to pound wooden stakes into the red earth. Since then I've heard less colorful stories about the mission's inception. I don't know which story is true, but I know the one I prefer, if the mission had to exist at all. What I do know is that the mission caused great losses and damage to many Navajo and Zuni children and their families, and also to white children like me.

I date the beginning of my awareness of the injustices among whites and Native people earlier than my time at Rehoboth. It goes back to 1952, the year that I turned four. It was shortly after my father received his assignment as a missionary in Shiprock, New Mexico. At that time, Shiprock was a tiny village in the northern section of the Navajo Nation, an emblem of colonization, since nothing had existed there before the US Government established it as one of its administrative locations. Our church's mission board provided us with a large two-story house in Shiprock. It stood on a hill, and from our living room, a large picture window looked down across a road onto the activity surrounding Jack's Trading Post. Standing at the window was like watching a movie, although I had never seen a movie at the time, so I would not have drawn that comparison then.

Navajo people drove up to Jack's from miles around in horse-drawn wagons to unload bags of wool and piñon nuts, carefully folded rugs, silver and turquoise jewelry wrapped in flour sacking. They walked into the trading post with these and came out with bags of Bluebird flour slung over shoulders, cans of Folgers coffee, loops of rope, enamel basins, bags of sugar. After loading these into their wagons, some stood against the trading post walls or in the shade of gnarled cottonwoods exchanging news while their horses nosed into feedbags.

Sometimes visitors came to us from God's great Midwest. My parents treated them with deference because they supported the mission with money and prayers. During one of these visits, I was playing on the floor in the living room, and the visitors stood at the picture window, watching the scene below them. One of them said, "Just look at those Indians down there."

I said without hesitation and a knife in my voice, "They're not Indians. They're nice Navajos." I'm sure I knew that Diné (Navajos' name for themselves) could be called Indians; I objected to the tone I heard. I didn't know the word racism, but I didn't need to know it. I knew what I heard, and I didn't have to think at all about how I felt. I recognized the sound of injustice. I knew it was up to me to correct it.

No doubt my parents were embarrassed and scolded me for disrespecting adults. I hope the Midwesterners were discomfited by a child's righteous indignation. I wasn't punished, but I would have felt hurt because my mother and father misunderstood my intent.

My first playmates on the hill, Rudy and Bobby Yellowhair, lived in a white canvas tent close by our imposing, gray and brown house. They lived there year-round with their mother Iva. In Shiprock, temperatures before climate change ranged on average from fifteen degrees Fahrenheit in winter to ninety-four degrees in summer. Someone had tried to make the tent withstand the weather better by nailing discarded slabs of wood ammunition boxes around its walls. In winter the tent was heated by a woodstove whose smoke pipe snaked up through a hole in the tent roof.

When it snowed, I worried about my friends. "Aren't they cold?" I asked. Quite possibly my parents offered Iva mittens and sweaters and caps with earflaps from the mission barrel. But I knew that tent couldn't be as warm as our house with its lovely radiant wall heaters. I didn't know the word privilege, but I knew there was an imbalance. I knew something was wrong, and I felt helpless about it.

When our class moved up to fifth grade at the mission school, a boy who had already done fifth grade joined us. Even the second time around, that grade was a struggle for Tom. And all the grades after that until our senior year, which was when Tom finally blossomed. We all got to see then how smart he really was. That was the year in which he at last mastered English, and everything else fell into place. That was the year I truly understood what it meant to come to school speaking no English, punished for speaking the only language you had. I wondered how my classmates had functioned at all. Later I understood that they had received no special instruction in the learning of a second language. This was not language teaching through a carefully sequenced immersion strategy; it was sink or swim at the level of native speakers.

When our teachers at the mission school assigned written work in high school, some of my friends asked me to edit theirs. I was glad to do it, but sometimes I worried that the teachers would think we were cheating. Later I learned the word paternalism, and at that point, I wondered if being a helper had been paternalistic. I wanted things to be equal, and maybe they were. The friend who most often asked me to edit her work had been a playmate when we were kids. She was the one who gave me my first Navajo cake from a girl's kinaalda, her puberty ceremony, sharing with me a bit of the culture in which I was learning to live. We had ridden bikes together around the sheep dip and had sleepovers in each other's homes. Maybe it's not possible to measure equality in a friendship because the exchanges are both different and the same.

All these things I saw and heard and lived with, and more and more I knew that something was wrong. I didn't have the words racism, privilege, paternalism, but I knew the reality from deep within, and I knew something needed to change. I just didn't know what or how or if it was up to me to do anything. Still in high school, I had arguments with my father about some of these things for which I had no words. I thought, especially after seeing how Tom and some of my other friends transformed along the way, that education was the answer, an equalizer. Education and love. It all came down to love, I thought. I said this one Sunday afternoon, and my father said, "Ach! You talk too much about love!"

I shot back, "How can I talk too much about love when the Bible says that God is love?" I stalked off on the high heels of Sunday, no love for my father in that moment.

In a recent interview with Terry Gross, David Oyelowo, a British actor of Nigerian descent, said of African Americans, if "your history is rooted in slavery, that really, I think, messes with your sense of self...." The same case might be made for the emotional impact of conquest and colonization on Native peoples—that the less tangible effects on a sense of self are passed on from historical times to the present.

Recent studies confirm Oyelowo's intuitive understanding. They show that trauma is carried from generation to generation on the double helix of DNA. So the soul-crushing trauma suffered by the ancestors of my indigenous friends lives on in them. Some of my friends have told me stories about things that happened to grandparents and great grandparents—The Long Walk of 1864 and the return in 1868, lost land, lost language. The list goes on. What happened at Rehoboth in the early 20th century is experienced not only through stories passed down, but those events are also borne on the genes.

Indignities continue today. Indigenous students are routinely forbidden to adorn graduation caps with beadwork or feathers. Male students with long braids have been suspended pending haircuts. The Washington Redskins and their fans refuse to drop their racist name. A national news anchor announces the patent ridiculousness that Natives are illegal aliens. In some states, public school curricula teach that Native people are gone from the surface of the Earth, that they are people of the past.

On the bright side, genetic research also suggests that resilience rides on the genes from the fathers and mothers to the children and grandchildren. Attend a powwow, and you will see ample evidence of a vibrant, thriving indigenous culture. I have friends who are master weavers of traditional rugs and sashes as well as users of new fiber art techniques combined with ancient methods and themes. I know painters who bring together current and past subjects with bold new styles and methods. Former colleagues work with intense love and creativity to keep the Diné language alive in the minds and mouths of Navajo youth.

Despite the resilience, I am overcome by the deep knowledge that something is wrong, and it is not about Natives. Nor is it about non-Natives, rightfully called by some Natives illegal immigrants. It is about relationship. It is about brokenness. It is about a once bright potential for living in harmony that has been smashed by genocide, both cultural and actual.

The year 2003 saw the 100th anniversary of the mission at Rehoboth. Missionaries among indigenous people are infamous for working hand-in-glove with governments to "pacify" or "civilize" indigenous people. After "The only good Indian is a dead Indian," came the phrase, "Kill the Indian, save the man." And that was where missionaries came into the picture. I knew that Rehoboth's centennial celebration would include recognition of the damage the missionaries had caused to Navajo and Zuni people, as well as an apology.

In righteous anger about incalculable damage, passed on to generations of those 1903 and subsequent

Rehoboth students, I refused to attend the celebration. I believed that the apology would constitute a sort of whitewash (pun intended), a theater piece enacted so that the mission could go on doing what it had done before, only more humanely now and with a lightened conscience. Admittedly the school had changed markedly for the better since my friends and I were students. Instead of punishing students for speaking their mother tongue, being part of the elimination of the language, the school now taught Diné language classes, thus becoming part of the general language revitalization effort. The mission had built a communications center honoring the Navajo Code Talkers of World War II. But to me this seemed to be too little too late. A Diné friend and colleague of mine would not even go to the mission for her mother's funeral in pain-filled protest. I saw my refusal to attend the celebration as an act of solidarity with her and others. And when I say that the mission intended to go on doing what it had been doing, I mean that it would continue proselytizing for Christianity—something I object to strongly.

My seven brothers did attend the celebration, including the reconciliation service, though reconciliation is really a misnomer. Conciliation would be a more accurate word, since reconciliation implies that there was once harmony that needs only to be restored between whites and Natives, when in fact such harmony never existed. During the ceremony Rehoboth's executive director, a Navajo church leader, and the director of the denomination's mission board offered public admissions of guilt accompanied by apologies. They called their formal words "A Message of Confession and Reconciliation." Then there was time for responses from former students and parents. I heard about it all from my brothers.

One of them told me about a Navajo woman I'd known since fourth grade. Carol was a year ahead of me in school. My brother said, "She got up and started crying. She said, 'I didn't think this day would ever come.'"

I felt some shame. Maybe I had been wrong. Perhaps the apology was more sincere than I had imagined. Or maybe the degree of sincerity had mattered less than the fact that an attempt at conciliation had been made at all, the recognition that an apology was needed. I have often said in situations that are far less grave—for example, when a retail worker apologizes to me, "Sorry goes a long ways with me." Maybe it was like that.

It is only right that churches, perpetrators of some of the gravest transgressions upon people who were once truly sovereign in their own land, should be some of the first to attempt conciliation. These are good and necessary beginnings. But the need for conciliation extends far beyond apologies from religious groups. The most well-known and largest government-sponsored truth and reconciliation process occurred in South Africa following the end of Apartheid. The people who conducted and participated in the truth and reconciliation process often did feel overwhelmed. One way that they dealt with the enormity of the task was to set limits—limits as to who would testify in public hearings and what forms reparations might take. Often reparation was a token or it was creatively applied to a group. The process was not without its flaws and critics, but as Desmond Tutu, the head of the commission, has reiterated, it allowed South Africa to make a transition to majority rule without the bloodshed that has occurred in so many other places following similar changes.

Fania Davis Jordan, in her Yes Magazine article, cites a few government-sponsored truth and reconciliation processes that have occurred in North America. The first to happen in the US was the Greensboro Truth and Reconciliation Commission in North Carolina, held in 2004 and focusing on actions by the Ku Klux Klan in 1979. Maine has an ongoing truth commission initiated by the state's governor and indigenous leaders to address the forced assimilation of Native children in the state's welfare system. The Truth and Reconciliation Commission of Canada, only recently completed, has undertaken a much larger effort regarding the abuses of First Nations people (as indigenous people are called in Canada) in residential schools. Even though the Canadian commission addressed a nationwide injustice, it had a limited focus—that of boarding school wrongs. Other commissions named by

Jordan also limited their scope, and that may be the best way to begin a process of conciliation. As Martin Luther King, Jr., said, "Unless we learn to live together as brothers [and sisters] we will die together as fools."

It was social media that put me back in touch with many of the Diné friends with whom I'd lost contact. It was also social media that made me intensely aware of the level of pain and anger most of them are still living with. In addition, I see the strength, the ability to bounce back (or forward), the commitment to a healthful lifeway, the willingness to engage with joy and humor.

It was also social media that confronted me daily with the ongoing insults and long-lived wounds that my friends experienced. Every single time I read of them, I think, "Something has to change. We can't just go on like this, in this discord, this rupture between Natives and the rest of us—discord that most of the rest of us aren't even aware exists. That's got to be the first step—awareness."

The powerful sense that something must change motivated me to study truth and reconciliation processes that others—churches, governments, and individuals—have undertaken. In 2009, President Obama signed into law an official apology to Native people. In the words of the bill's sponsor, then Senator Sam Brownback (R-KS), the purpose of the Native American Apology Resolution was "to officially apologize for the past ill-conceived policies by the US Government toward the Native Peoples of this land and re-affirm our commitment toward healing our nation's wounds and working toward establishing better relationships rooted in reconciliation." It is always important to recognize beginnings, however small, in a healing process. However, such apologies do not go nearly far enough.

The healing model that seems most common is quite simple. It begins by giving those who have been wounded and also their descendants the opportunity to tell their stories, to tell what happened to them and their ancestors. Then the actual perpetrators or the representatives of the perpetrators acknowledge the offenses, take responsibility and offer their sorrow for what happened. Direct perpetrators must then change their behavior, and when institutions and governments are involved, reparations are necessary along with the changes. Reparations are most often thought of as monetary, but, as in South Africa, other types of restitution may be more meaningful and practical.

Before I grasped this paradigm, I was always at a loss for words when my friends posted images and words in social media about horrible injustices and insults, past and present. I felt that anything I could say would be of little value, so I said nothing. Finally, finding a guide for conciliation showed me how to respond, how I must respond at every opportunity, whether face-to-face or in writing.

My first chance came when a former colleague posted a photographic triptych on Facebook. The top two were sepia-tone boarding school photos. On the left were Native children with long hair wearing a blend of traditional and Anglo dress, looking angry. On the right they had shorn hair (boys) or hair pulled back in neat, tight buns (girls) and wore uniforms; they looked subdued, "pacified," as they used to say. Below these two was a color photo of whites at a sporting event, decked out in feathered headdresses and face paint. The text read, "WERE THEY FORCED TO GIVE UP THEIR CULTURE SO YOU COULD DO THIS?"

I commented on my friend's post, "Thank you for posting this. I want you to know that I am deeply sorry for the damage that my people did and continue to do to your people. Deeply. We need conciliation."

My friend replied almost immediately, "Thank you, Anna." She added a heart emoticon, and I started to cry, really cry. Hard. Clearly, when there is a societal wound, we are all wounded and in need of healing.

My next opportunity to extend myself in a gesture of conciliation also took place online. A friend had posted the following quote by the late South African singer and civil rights activist, Miriam Makeba:

> *The conqueror writes history; they came, they*

conquered, they write. You don't expect people who came to invade us to write the truth about us. They will always write negative things about us and they have to do that because they have to justify their invasion in all countries.

I replied:

Thank you for posting this. I love Miriam Makeba and her music, too. More important here and now, thank you for posting her words about colonists and revisionist history to justify the invasion and occupation. I am deeply sorry for the pain and damage my people caused and continue to cause to your people. I hope for and want to work toward conciliation.

I had been more hesitant when I wrote this comment, less sure of the response I might get because I have sensed more anger from Jennie, whom I'd known in our mission boarding school days, than from my former colleague. Sometimes I had felt that the anger might be directed at me, although it is often hard to know for sure about emotions when the communication is online rather than in person.

A few hours after I posted my response, my friend "liked" my reply. Several hours later she wrote, "Anna, thank you for being an ally."

I happen to be a member of a sexual minority, and I know from a deep place how essential it is to have allies in my life and in the lives of my tribe. Once again, I was moved to tears. Jennie's response was confirmation that I could begin where I was and take advantage of every chance I had. It has to start somewhere. I was saying, "I hear your pain. I want to respond. I want to be part of a healing process. I don't know how it will look, but I want to do it." I know that each time I will be improvising, relying upon the experience of those who entered this process before me. Every time I responded to a friend's pain at having been injured by my people, I learned something new about the process. Jennie's two-step response, several hours apart taught me that it can take time for someone to absorb and respond to a reconciling effort.

A few weeks later Alice Whitegoat, a close friend, and I went for a walk in a Russian olive and cottonwood forest. Scattered among the trees lay small meadows, thick with foxtails and Queen Anne's lace. At one point we sat on a bench beside the path, and in the course of our conversation I asked her about her parents' decision not to speak the Diné language with her when she was growing up. I wasn't surprised to learn that a doctor at Rehoboth had given them advice that became the deciding factor.

We started walking again, and I took a deep breath after a short internal debate. "Alice, I've never said this to you before, but I am deeply sorry for the damage that my people have caused your people." We were walking side-by-side, but we paused and faced each other, and my mouth and voice started trembling. I felt tears coming. I didn't want that, didn't want to make Alice uncomfortable in any way, and I knew that my visible emotion could do that.

Alice seemed taken aback and made excuses for me. "It's not your responsibility. You were just a child." I think she meant that as a child, I had had no more power in my situation than any of my Navajo friends had had in theirs.

I knew there was an answer regarding my responsibility, but I couldn't think of how to say it, except for the Bible verse about the sins of the fathers being visited upon the children for generations to come. I didn't want to use that, in part because of our mutual mission school background, so I kept silent and the moment passed.

Of course what I needed to say came to me after we had left the forest and parted ways. It was this: "We're all in this together. Whether it's something we've inherited from way back, whether we are dealing it out or receiving it now. We're all in it. We're all affected by it. So we're all responsible for doing the healing work. All of us." We are not only all responsible; we are all in need of it. Desmond and Mpho Tutu point out in The Book of Forgiving, "To walk the path of forgiveness is to recognize that your crimes harm you as they harm me. To walk the path of forgiveness is to recognize that my dignity is bound up in your dignity, and every wrongdoing hurts us all."

Talking with Alice in person offered what may have been the most important learning experience in personal conciliation I'd had by then. From it, I drew the conclusion that a face-to-face engagement probably requires some preparation. I could have seen this from Jennie's online response, which gave her all the time she needed, and from the fact that her response came in stages. I think when I am physically with someone, we must have an agreement that we are mutually entering a process with the goal of making things better. An agreement implies a more formal process, not something I might say off the cuff, as I did with Alice. At the very least, we need to be seated, making direct contact. It didn't help Alice that I got visibly and audibly emotional in that context, but if we had first agreed to talk about it, it might have been okay. As it was, I got the feeling that my attempt was just a source of embarrassment for her.

Another factor could be Alice's age and the mellowing that has taken place in her and that I've witnessed over the years. I think she has come to terms with many personal injuries, that she has in many ways moved beyond them, taking her own route to get there.

I have attempted the beginnings of personal conciliation a few more times. One of those attempts gave me even more information, although I'm not sure how to use it yet. I followed the same steps of acknowledging the damage, apologizing, and making a commitment to conciliation after a friend posted a disturbing meme about Hitler having admired and been influenced by the mass extermination of indigenous people in the US. My friend did not reply to my comment. But two days later he thanked me publicly in social media for a gift that had been given several years earlier. I felt as though this was an indirect reply, and it has caused me to question the advisability of attempting online resolution to these gaping wounds. Improvisation most often involves trial and error.

The next question I ask myself is, "Where do I go from here, from these small, individual attempts?" As

I told Jennie, I want to work for conciliation. I am convinced that individual efforts are needed, but they are not enough. On the other hand, the thought of trying to have an effect on the bigger picture is daunting. I keep reminding myself that others are already doing this work and that I don't have to do it alone. I've asked myself if I might join an existing group or find others who would want to engage in the work with me. I have also wondered if writing about conciliation—to make others aware of the need—might fulfill my obligation. It seems too little.

In addition to the question about responsibility, I have felt compelled to ask if I have a right to assert the need for conciliation. Should the impetus be coming from Native people, not from me? African American Ava DuVernay wrote, "I'm interested in having people of color at the center of their own lives. We don't need to be saved by anyone. We do not need to have anyone sweeping in on a white horse or someone saving the day or assisting us in our own narrative."

"No," I reply mentally. "That is certainly not what is needed. Conciliation has to be an act of mutuality, of complementarity—healing for people on all sides. Otherwise, it will fail." I hasten to add that I only saw that short snippet from DuVernay, and I may well be applying it out of her intended context, but her words fueled my thoughts about what might be an appropriate role for me in a conciliation process.

I brought up the idea of a Truth and Conciliation Commission with Alice Whitegoat. "Do you think the motivation for a commission needs to come from a Native person? Do I have a right to work to make it happen?"

Without pausing, she said, "You have a right because you're a human being."

Right. Responsibility. Perhaps even joy. Kate Bornstein in Gender Outlaw writes, "Your life's work begins where your great joy meets the world's great hunger." Maybe this is what engaging in truth and conciliation work will be for me. Great joy. Perhaps it is not an obligation; perhaps it will be an oblation offered in joy.

In August of 2014, I attended the First Annual Indigenous Fine Art Market in Santa Fe. The day was chilly, gray and rainy, but spirits were high. The art, from all over the US and Canada, was powerful and haunting in its blend of the traditional with the avant-garde. Entertainment reflected that blend—break dancing, traditional hoop dances, time-honored musical groups and contemporary ones that mixed it up with both humor and gravitas.

Certain paintings sliced deep, bringing tears and sometimes laughter. I enjoyed conversations with artists about their work. I met with friends, shared food and coffee, sauntered with them among the booths. What struck me most powerfully, what I kept coming back to, was how this market, this festival of art and engagement, could serve as a model for a new way of being with one another. Every imaginable color of human was present—red, brown, beige, mahogany, gold, coffee, pink, butterscotch, blue-black, cream, rose, copper—strolling, laughing, talking. I never once saw a moment of conflict while I sat on a low stone wall with my friends and watched humanity stream by—babies, crones bent with age, youth with dreadlocks, young men wearing the traditional Navajo bun, the bitsii'yeel. Clothing represented Africa, the Middle East, indigenous America, and including dramatic couture that combined ancient themes with contemporary invention. I saw people from every continent on Earth, every racial strand and mix, enjoying, appreciating, learning from one another. Joying in each other's differences and commonality.

I thought, "This is how it could be. This is how we humans—the only race there is—how we need to be." That day gave me a vision filled with sounds and stunning images—a vision for a new way of being with one another in the US, across colors, shapes, sizes, ideals. But it was only a dream, a dream I would even have to call sentimental, if I don't find some way to be part of making it surpass meager happy thoughts of sisterhood and brotherhood.

Art & Photography

Running Colors, Acrylic
Elaine Gerard

After The War, photograph
Aaron Ireland

Country Cloth Days, photograph
Aaron Ireland

Ritual Masks, photograph
Aaron Ireland

Bags to Go, photograph
Aaron Ireland

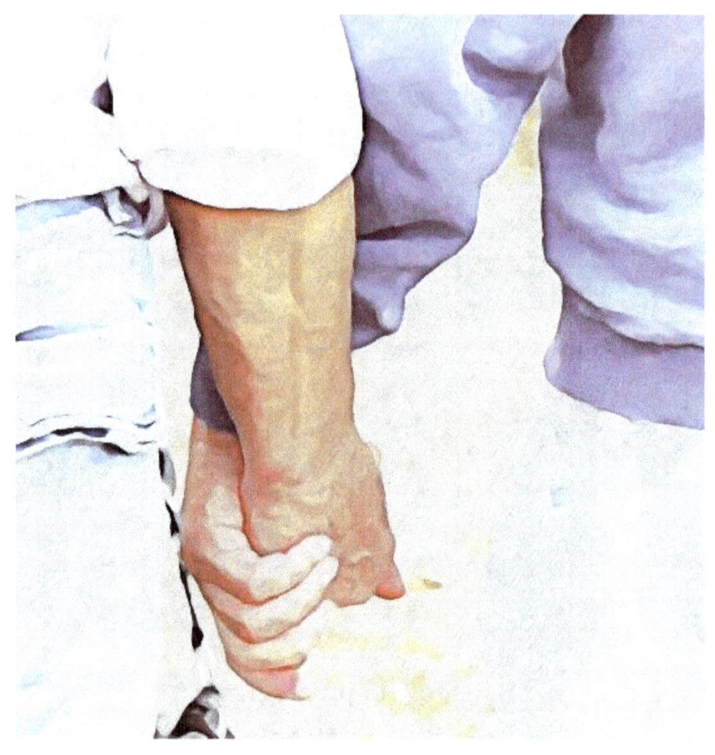

Have A Little Faith, Multi-Media
Paula Dawn Lietz

Against All Odds, Photograph
Paula Dawn Lietz

We Are Our Own Masons, Mixed-Media
Paula Dawn Lietz

Integrity, Mixed-Media
Paula Dawn Lietz

When We Are SmallFeather Rest, Photograph
Laura Matthias Bendoly

This image, "Feather Rest," shows a swan asleep at the Columbus Zoo. It was tightly wrapped up in its plumage – but then woke, and stretched, as we all do, ready to tend to its family and its duty as a mate. So elegant, so refined, such perfection and energy and freedom all compacted into the frame of my lens. The opulent white along the curve of the feather filaments, they layer life and seasons and cycles all atop one another. And yet, within a few years, this swan will die, passing on that astonishing perfection to another generation of birds. What freedom, what peace, what amazing universality. May we each gain strength of purpose in the utter non-self-absorption of the swan asleep, the peace of we breathless mortals looking on.

~Laura Matthias Bendoly

Tournesol, Photograph
Laura Matthias Bendoly

My photo, "Tournesol," shows the under side of a sculpted sunflower at Inniswood Metro Gardens in Westerville, Ohio. My image reflects the DoveTales theme in that these flower petals, like a dove's wing, can be seen from above and below as a kind of shelter. They, the petals and wings, are emblems of flight, of protection, of transcendence. They are unique and yet very familiar. The petals on the sculpture I shot show, too, how a momentary experience — the observation of a flower in bloom — can last an entire lifetime, when cast onto the photographic lens, or made into glass. Even after the dove has flown or the flower has wilted, the photograph remains. And the light that penetrates through these glass petals radiates out to the viewer, casting a shaded, welcome, motherly embrace.

~Laura Matthias Bendoly

A commentary on the United States' current immigration policies, I've titled my photographs "DACA Series (Deferred Action for Childhood Arrivals)." We read about the extraordinary numbers—of families torn apart through deportation to countries where their lives are in danger, children separated from their parents and left without nurturing for weeks or months on the concrete floors of inhumane detention centers, and families living in fear who work, contribute to our society, and pay more taxes than our president—but they are more than numbers. They are human beings, like our own families, with histories and love and hope and dreams, and they are carrying this trauma forward in ways that they, and we, will pay for indefinitely.

~Carmel Mawle

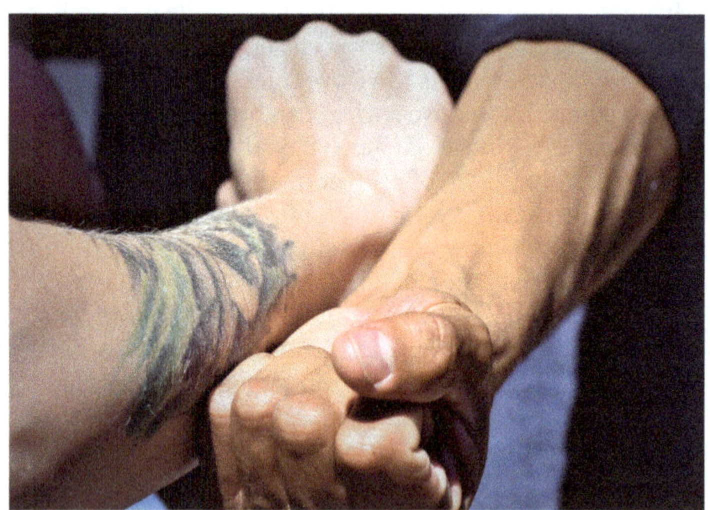

Colors, Photograph
Carmel Mawle

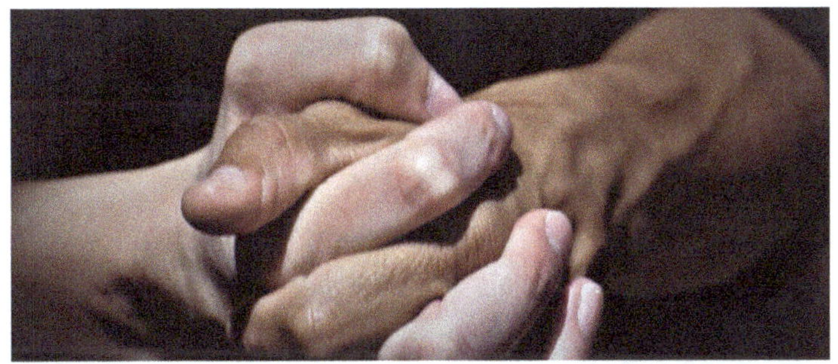

Entwined, Photograph
Carmel Mawle

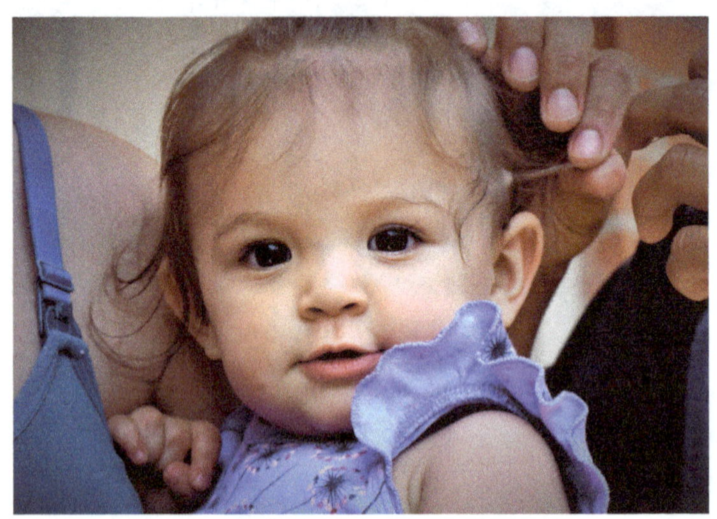

Family, Photograph
Carmel Mawle

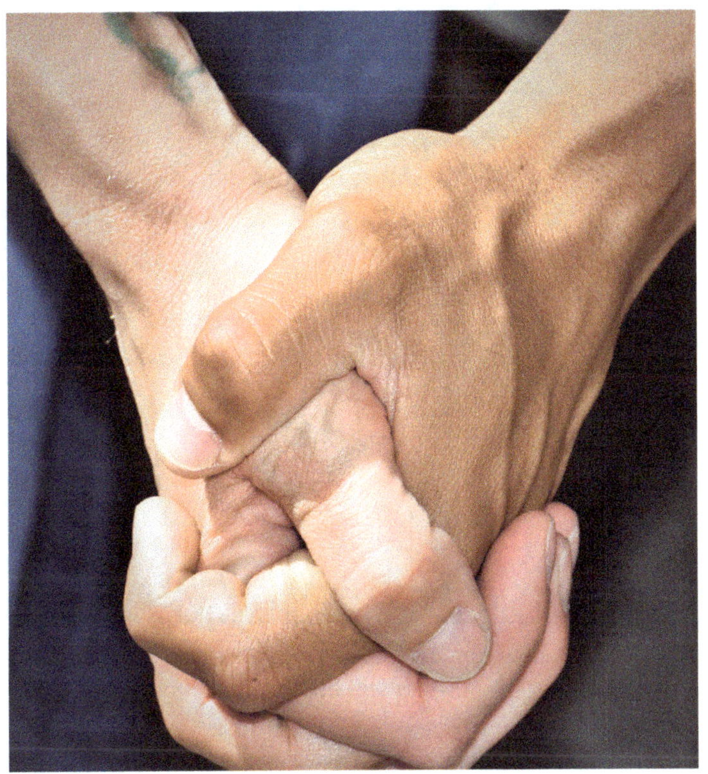

Family, Photograph
Carmel Mawle

Mother and Child, Photograph
Carmel Mawle

Sidewalk Market in Monrovia 1
Vermon Washington

Sidewalk Market in Monrovia 2
Vermon Washington

Kehkeh in Monrovia

Vermon Washington

2019 Young Writers Contest Winners

Participating in the Writing for Peace Young Writers Contest takes a commitment to research, an open mind, and refining the craft of writing. Entries from across the globe exemplified this commitment, and many of our young writers are working in a second language. Many thanks to the teachers and mentors who encouraged, inspired, and guided them to prepare their best work. This year we are excited to welcome writers from the Philippines, Morocco, and Japan, joining other forward thinking future leaders from a total of 27 countries. We're so happy to share their work with you now!

In Poetry~

First Place: Sharvari Deshpande from Pune, Maharashtra, India, for "In The Valleys of Kashmir."

Second Place: Emmy Song from Rockville, Maryland, U.S. for "A Walk Down Lafayette Street."

Third Place: Sarah Street from Atlanta, Georgia, U.S. for "Earth."

In Fiction~

First Place: Lucas Tucker from Moraga, California, U.S. for "Cleanse Your Nation."

Second Place: Sally Liu from Holzheim, Germany, for "7,000 miles."

Third Place: EbunOluwa Ojebode from Ibadan, Oyo, Nigeria, for "Male ears, Dead End."

In Nonfiction~

First Place: Christina Wang from Roswell, Georgia, U.S. for "Bringing Gender Back: How the Japanese Youth Connect With Their Culture By Foregoing Gender Norms."

Second Place: Eunice Lee from Seoul, South Korea, for "When a Mommy Becomes a Nanny."

Third Place: Junwon Lee from Seoul, South Korea, for "The Small but Mighty Survivors."

Sharvari Deshpande
First Place, Poetry
"In The Valleys of Kashmir"
Grade, SYBA, S P College
Pune, Maharashtra, India

"To begin with, I am an artist and I love to express myself through my paintings. But there was a point in my life when I was feeling low and that is when writing, through the medium of words, came to me as a supporting friend. I began writing by expressing myself, and then I started to elucidate my feelings about my surroundings and social issues through it.

"I aspire to be a civil servant, so that one day I have the authority to bring change in the society and work for its betterment. I want to help those children dream who cannot afford to dream in their current conditions. And that is my ultimate goal.

"I feel that my writings and the work that I will do in my future can contribute to bring this change and make someone's tomorrow better!

"I've never been to the state of Kashmir. I know Kashmir is an integral part of India yet the people there aren't experiencing what other fellow Indians are – Freedom. Whatever I know is through the articles and news. And yet, even though it is a disputed land I feel it's like my home. A land I care about. People I care about. I live in a very safe environment. Children of my age there don't.

"This taught me to thank the universe for this life which seems like a luxury."

In The Valleys of Kashmir

Snowflakes on the red ground
And bullets instead of flowers
Paradise on earth now not found
And the land prone to blood showers

Tiny eyes and pink cheeks
Land of beauty, now a warzone
Afraid little minds witnessing terrible weeks
Facing the odds, all alone

Deprived of opportunities, dwindled ambitions
Their home, once a heaven
Destroyed for conceited reasons
History of their land in complications woven

Thousands of lives trapped in political games
Recalled only on some important dates
Responsibility of none, yet too many claims
Just a line on paper, deciding their fates

Life of normalcy, a cherished dream
Their present is occupied by terror
Tears demanding the freedom they have never seen
Is this our country's true mirror?

Emmy Song
Second Place, Poetry
"A Walk Down Lafayette Street"
Grade 11, Montgomery Blair High School
Rockville, Maryland, U.S.

Emmy Song is a writer and high school student from Rockville, Maryland. She speaks out about social issues, such as gun violence and women's rights, through poetry and journalism. Her poems have been published in various print and online publications, including Blue Marble Review, Sierra Nevada Review, and Rattle Young Poet Anthology. When she isn't writing, Emmy advocates for gender equality in STEM fields and dabbles in videography. She intends to study applied mathematics and creative writing in college, and later use her education and skills to continue pushing for social justice.

a walk down lafayette street

Girl in a white dress tracing steps
she's taken a thousand times, but every
time her legs tremble a little harder and
breath catches a little faster. She walks
in linear time, maintains constant velocity
to upkeep a mask of surety, beating on
against the friction between past and
future. Because when she's a blur of
movement, the world is in limbo and
her luck cannot run out. Foreign shadows,
abrasive stubble, and smoked cigarettes
lurking around corners—this and the
crude weight of a drunkard are what she
fears. Her topography, the delicate
folds of her cotton dress, to rob them
would be sacrilege. And she continues
walking, borne forward by pure conviction
that the rise and fall of the sun will keep
her safe, as it had in the past. Friction
distorts, past and present future fuse,
and girl, like arrow, still ceaseless.

Sarah Street
Third Place, Poetry
"Earth."
Grade 10, The Westminster Schools
Atlanta, Georgia, U.S.

"Many of my works delve into issues of social justice, especially pertaining to the worldwide refugee crisis. After taking a class on children's human rights last year, my world perspective altered significantly. I decided to use my writing as a forum to invoke change and spread a message about the plights that children endure today."

Sarah Street is a rising junior and Writing Fellow at the Westminster Schools in Atlanta, where she also writes for the school newspaper and edits the literary magazine. Her poetry has been featured or is forthcoming in Aerie International, Just Poetry National Quarterly, Live Poet's Society, and TeenInk among others. Sarah's work has been recognized by The New York Times Student Poetry Contest, the Scholastic Art and Writing Awards, and the River of Words Poetry Project. She recently participated in the 2019 Kenyon Review Young Writers workshop. Sarah's writing frequently explores themes of children's rights and social justice; she is passionate about promoting diversity, advocating for human rights, and inspiring unity through writing, music, and community service.

Earth

An unprecedented 68.5 million people around the world have been forced from home. Among them are nearly 25.4 million refugees, over half of whom are under the age of 18.
-UNHCR

The girl wakes up to another newly birthed sky, another elsewhere.

Her cheek rests on her father's angular back,

carved out of the familiar rumble of houses

crumbling into ash. The girl knows the rumble –

finds comfort in its persistence. She doesn't know much,

but she knows that only the lost truly know the world.

Her mother faints, hammers her head into the grass,

making some kind of mark. Maybe not the right one.

If this is their Earth, then why isn't it home?

Eventually they find camp in a corrupt Turkish town,

where a jagged emptiness pollutes thick factory smoke.

Paths lined with garbage become red carpets-

Murky puddles mock the dead stars.

Once the clock breaks again,

when the grass grows red

and the trees revoke their shade,

the footprints press deeper.

Step

Repeat

Step

Repeat.

Lucas Tucker
First Place, Fiction
"Cleanse Your Nation"
Grade 10, Head-Royce School
Moraga, California, U.S.

"I believe that writing, like playing guitar or painting a picture, is a way to communicate emotions and ideas to others through various senses. When I found the 2019 Young Writers Contest through some online research, I felt it would be a great opportunity to expose people to the vast amount of antisemitism in modern day America. By writing this piece, I was able to express deeper emotions that I cannot express to friends and my community.

"As part of my 10th grade English class, I learned about the plight of Japanese-Americans during their World War II Internment. Reading about the prejudice that this population faced inspired me to empathize with my own Jewish community, and get very deep into the day to day struggles that American Jews face. I ran into many challenges throughout this writing process, and focusing on the hate and prejudice really forced me to expand my writing skills. While I am still figuring out my career path, I hope to continue connecting people of different backgrounds and cultures through writing, computer science, and shared human experiences."

Cleanse Your Nation

Alright, I admit it. You are right. You were always right. I was the one behind the scenes, controlling the government without anyone knowing. I started a business and unfairly floated to the top of the social ladder, along with all of the others like me. How did you know I want it so much? I make so much of it as your deli waiter, your local kombucha business owner, your pharmacist... but I am also more. I am the one you see in the news, stealing from the poor. I'm the kosher meat producer. I am the one profiting off both political parties. I am the president of the United States, but you never see me. I am the curly haired mother in her sixties, gossiping in your local delicatessen. What a klutz. I am your challah maker in the bakery on the corner who always says "oy vey" when they spill an ingredient. I am the one with the big nose, waiting to make a deal. How did you figure it out? I am the one that sleeps atop bags filled with green paper, dreaming about the exploitation of your economy. I live silently among you. I am simply biding my time before I can interfere with your business and uproot all that hard work that you have been putting in day after day. I must be the source of your failure.

You never saw me but you knew I was there. You were always right about achieving power, the dream of my people, that I am proud to say that I have fulfilled. It was not hard to steal all of your data, to take away all your wages so that you could barely afford to feed your family. The goal is just not that complicated; I simply want to dominate America's hierarchy and steal from all others. I transfer currency from your bank account to mine because I am the CEO of that bank. Before you turn on the faucet, remember that I make a profit because I own the utility company. Before you eat, remember that you are helping me pay for a new mansion in Israel, because I own the company that cultivated that food. A mansion in Jerusalem? Why not. Before you sleep, remember that I inherited the business that makes your mattress. Let's double the price, the goyim will never know.

You cannot get me out of your life or your country, for I will always be everywhere. Just when you think you have finally succeeded in your marriage, your business, or with your nation as a whole, remember that am snickering in the back room, because I have already devised a master plan to strip from you all that you hold dear.

So there, now you know my little secret. I do not care what you do about it anymore. Split up my whole family. Take my pets and my grandparents. Smash my childhood wooden guitar. Bomb my house after you remove all value from it. Stacks of green paper hidden in the walls. Command your army to put my people away forever, so that we may not add to the already irreversible damage done to you. Take it, take me. Vanquish my people from your country like you would maggots from an organic fruit. Make sure that I never succeed again.

It's over. Can I leave now?

Sally Liu
Second Place, Fiction
"7,000 miles"
Grade 12, Albert-Einstein-Gymnasium
Holzheim, Germany

Sally Liu is an 18-year-old student from Germany. She has been fascinated by reading and writing for as long as she can remember and enjoys writing short stories, poems and songs that capture and reflect her feelings and thoughts. Aside from writing, she is also passionate about music and sports. Sally loves singing, playing the piano and she has recently started teaching herself to play the guitar. She also enjoys running, being outside and spending time with her friends.

This is the second time that she has participated in the Young Writer's Contest. Writing for Peace has given her the opportunity to express her feelings and personal experiences and to reach out to like-minded people all over the world – a dream she has pursued ever since she took up writing.

Having passed her final exams last month, Sally will begin studying pharmacy in Zurich this autumn.

Sally Liu

7,000 Miles

A letter to my grandmother, written from my mother's perspective

Mother,

I am writing this in an attempt to apologize for something that cannot be righted by words, but right now, words are all I have.

Words and the hope that you will believe me when I say that I would have single-handedly walked these 7,000 miles, just to hold my own brother in his last moments. And even though you have always seen in him nothing but a disappointment, I know that you believe he did not deserve to die like this, suffering from terminal lung cancer without the doctors disclosing his diagnosis, getting thrown out of hospital for want of health insurance and being reanimated against his will, forced to sustain a life unworthy of this very term.

For, even though we are 7,000 miles apart, the universal love for our own children unites us, a love strongest felt when in fear of losing part of ourselves. Never have I been so aware of my love for Sally than when she developed an eating disorder five years ago, when she starved herself to the point of being hospitalized for her own safety. She was diagnosed with *anorexia nervosa,* but how can I even hope to make you understand that in a country providing what you would call "abundance" to its citizens, anybody would deliberately refrain from satisfying their most essential needs? Do you remember how we used to work for hours on the rice fields, overwhelmed with joy if we happened to get our hands on a bowl of rice, rather than sweet potatoes? But did you know that nowadays, the Germans have established a mentality of deeming sweet potatoes the angels of health whereas white rice is almost considered the direct path to hell?

I cannot grasp the whole complexity of Sally's

illness, but I am certain that this collision of obsessive health and beauty ideals on one side and the promotion of perfectionism on the other can easily tear a fragile heart apart. And she is not the only one.

With your son and only remaining companion gone, must not you feel as if being swallowed by an ocean of loneliness?

Because I do.

You probably think that I have everything because I live in a wealthy country with a social safety net that will catch me should I ever fall.

But what is all this money, this security to me? Can it repurchase the time I wish I had spent with my own father and brother? Can it protect me from losing yet another loved one, from losing you, without a chance of being there for you when you need me the most? I have never told you, but if I could remake but one decision in my life, it would be this: the decision of moving to Germany.

I often think of you and in my mind's eye, I see you sitting in your small flat, how you look out of the window for several hours, observing the children on their way to school.

Do you ever wish that you could turn back time? Or that you could at least freeze one moment and preserve it for eternity? That way, you never would have had to watch me leave China, and I would never have to watch my own children leave for university; you never would have been lonely all these years after Father died, and I would never have to face that same impending loneliness.

Here, in Germany, people often talk about the hardships faced by so-called "second-generation immigrants". But I don't see any of it in my own children, and for that I am grateful beyond words. Instead, I see a bright future awaiting them, a successful career, and, most importantly, a profound meaning in their lives. It has taken them some time to get there, but they do not feel torn between two worlds anymore; in fact, they have learned to cherish the gift of belonging to two worlds simultaneously, and being accepted by both.

But what about us?

Who bears the brunt of trying to reach for a cultural confluence that eludes one's grasp, if not us? Who understands what it is like to be confined to jobs way below one's skills, if not us?

Who feels truly torn, not between different universities but between different *universes,* if not us?

Everyone talks of being torn *between* different options, but no one seems to understand our struggles for what they are. They are not so much the result of a collision of different places, different people, different lives, even. They are part of a whole world within us, a world in which disparities are not social but emotional, where battles are fought not between conflicting nations but between conflicting values. I am torn not between, but *within.*

And I know you are, too. Sometimes I wonder whether it is meant to be like this; that, for everything that separates us, there will always be something that unites us.

You might not understand why such a bond would matter to me at all, because you are convinced that I already have everything you can only dream of. Yes, I have everything that money can buy, but without a home, everything is nothing. And sometimes, all I want to do is return to our dilapidated flat that is so rarely visited by the sun yet still glows like a beacon from my ocean's surface. To some, this place may seem like a prison; but to me, it is home.

Without your lullabies to guide me, I often find it hard to sleep. That is why every night, I look at the moon; and I find consolation in knowing that you are looking at the very same moon, that we are just on different sides of the same world.

Even so, I cannot help but wonder: if all that separates us are 7,000 miles...

then why does it feel like so much more?

EbunOluwa Ojebode
Third Place, Fiction
“Male ears, Dead End”
Grade 12, The International School
Ibadan, Oyo, Nigeria

“What I found disturbing about the Tiv culture was that they did not involve their women in decision making. The worst part is that the women have come to accept this. I used to view my culture as one in which the women made trouble about having equal rights. After this research, I now view women of my culture as strong independent women.”

Male Ears, Dead End

“PAAAAPAAAAAPAAAAA” “PAAAAPAAAAPAAA!” That was the village lookout, sounding the *kakaki* in a peculiar way. Everyone knew what this meant— the village was being attacked and it was time to flee. Chaos broke out.

“Yumam! Yumam,” women and children screamed.

Fulani herdsmen had attacked villages in Benue State for many years, but a few days ago, they had leveled Daudu, a neighboring village.

Dooshima was shaken to the bones as she heard the shouts of people. Like others, she had expected the attack to come in the night. Now, she was faced with a dilemma. From her father’s farm, she could safely flee to the next village, but that would mean leaving her family in danger. Amidst desperate cries, she headed for the market, the boiling point, to rescue her mother and siblings.

"Dooshima, where are you going? Everyone is dead, they behead anyone they see," her friend Targuma said, panting.

"I must go back! Mama and Papa are in the market, and my siblings are in the house."

"Shoo, Dooshima; no one is alive. You won't survive, let us go," Targuma pleaded.

Fired by filial love, Dooshima ran to the market, but it was no longer a market. Instead, it was a scene of pain. The slain lay still. The dying begged for help. Smoke oozed from the stalls.

"Shima!"

Dooshima turned sharply and there in the debris was her mother clutching her bleeding stomach.

"You have to flee now; they are heading to the farms to graze their cattle."

"No, Mama. I won't leave you. Mama, get up. We will make it!" She sobbed trying to no avail to lift her mother up. Both holding each other and crying. A strangled sound came from afar. She knew the herdsmen were close by. Her mother was coughing blood. Dooshima gasped as her mother pulled out the knife from her stomach and collapsed.

"Who is that?" One of the herdsmen shouted from the bush. Dooshima's eyes widened in horror. She had been spotted. Glancing at the dead body, she took to her heels, running with adrenaline as she could hear their footsteps close.

Passing through her uncle's mango farm, she knew she was close to home. Her sister's corpse, burnt huts, and more corpses were what was left in the compound. None were alive except ...

"Shima," a voice sounded. She turned, and there was her three-year old sister hiding in a big waterpot. She grabbed her and dashed for the bush, praying to God.

They ran towards her maternal uncle's village, just a thirty minute walk from hers, but when she reached her uncle's compound, there was no one around. *This must be a dream. Everyone has fled*, she thought, until she heard some noise behind her. The armed herdsmen again! She jumped into the nearby empty well, her sister tied to her back.

"Achi, achi!" Shima heard someone cough violently. Whoever it was, was on the verge of death. "Disciples, before I die, achi, you must kn ... know the secret of our survival. The day you attack a compound with Surumpu leaves, that day you would all die. Surumpu is a symbol of our ancestral covenant. Any compound with it must never be attacked!"

Shima knew the person who spoke was the bandits' leader. Her eyes widened in realization, she knew their secret.

Waiting till it was dark, Shima climbed out of the well, and began the long trek towards Anyiin, another village. Before leaving she had searched her uncle's house and taken some food items. When she reached Anyiin, she was immediately spotted and taken to the *Zaki Anyiin*. Due to her tiredness, she was allowed to rest till tomorrow before her questioning.

The next morning, a meeting was summoned with the village elders. With joy, Shima ran to the meeting place to tell them about the herdsmen's secret. Her message was simple: "plant Surumpu everywhere and we will never again be attacked!" Sadly, no one wanted to hear her.

"Woman? Who consults a woman in matters like this?" Taver, a muscular elder said. Everyone burst into laughter. "The day we begin to allow women to attend security meetings, that day I will cease to be a man," another man joined in. Louder laughter still.

"But ... but... our fathers, I have a solution to all our problems and pains," Dooshima begged.

"Hear that! If you had a solution, would your village be overrun? That is how a woman talks. Leave here now or else your head will part from your neck!"

Scared, Dooshima left. The men hissed, issuing

sterner threats against her and all women who did not know that they should be quiet and not meddle in security issues.

Over a period of two weeks, Dooshima made several attempts to talk to the men privately but as soon as she broached the subject, she was told to shut up, or even threatened! She spoke with elderly women but they told her not to bother because men do not listen to women.

And so it happened. Armed bandits in large numbers invaded Anyiin one dark night. The men fought gallantly but were overpowered. Many were slaughtered; many were raped. Anyiin was wiped out. Few escaped. As the dust settled, Dooshima spotted a badly wounded man and moved to help him. It was Taver.

"Why wouldn't you men listen to me?" Dooshima asked, tending Taver's wounds.

"Because we have male ears," Taver replied.

"But do you see now? Male ears lead to dead ends," Dooshima said.

Kakaki: an instrument that is blown when there is an attack.
Zaki Anyiin: Anyiin village head.
Yumam: save me

Christina Wang
First Place, Nonfiction
"Bringing Gender Back:
How the Japanese Youth Connect With Their Culture By Foregoing Gender Norms"
Grade 11, Milton High School
Roswell, Georgia, U.S

"I feel such unbridled enthusiasm for gender studies and equality. As someone who hates to conform to the status quo, I was compelled to write about an issue outside of the United States to give greater understanding to the way the agender/genderless community is perceived on a global scale.

"I want to become a writer when I grow up and perhaps go into journalism. Social activism will continue in my life some way, shape, or form."

Christina Wang is a student writer at Milton High School. She has been recognized by the Scholastic Art & Writing Competition. She was an Atlanta Youth Poet Laureate Finalist and has attended Kenyon Young Writers' 2019 Program. She is an editor at VOX Teen Communications, and has been published there as well as Crashtest Magazine, the Suoo Magazine; in her school's literature magazine, Globe; and on Teen Ink's website. She speaks four languages and lives her day to day life passionately. She is always in search of something interesting.

Bringing Gender Back: How the Japanese Youth Connect With Their Culture By Foregoing Gender Norms

In comparison to Japanese technological advancement exhibited through bullet trains and androids, overall social advancement with gender equality; LGBT acceptance; and, a mix of the two, genderless acceptance, appears slow. The Japanese stick to their heavily male-dominated ie system, from which their patriarchy seems to have evolved. Yet, the youth choose to forego such societal constructs and, with some, the gender binary altogether.

Define: The Nonbinary and What It Means In Japan

Interestingly enough, Japan holds a history with gender-bending actors and roles in traditional Noh, Kabuki, and Takarazuka theater. However, in the modern day, the nonbinary is most often associated with the Genderless Kei movement.

Genderless Kei

The Genderless Kei is a popular movement defined by its use of color and oversized clothing that young people, particularly around the Harajuku area, engage in, challenging the existing gender order through fashion. Participants are said to care about fashion and make-up without considering gender, achieving an androgynous look.

In an interview with i-D, Yutaro Goto, a charisma staff at a genderless boutique, states, "When I first wore a skirt, my dad was shocked. But after I explained to him how much I loved fashion, he has become very supportive."

Similarly Sasaki Toman, a model and pop band member, relates that his parents are both designers that encouraged him to dress differently in his interview with the New York Times. He believes that gender can exist, but doesn't have to exist.

In an article by Matthew Hernon, Satsuki Nakayama, model, mentions that, after she cut off her hair and threw out all her skirts, "her parents weren't as cool with the new look. Neither was her management, who was concerned that she would lose out on opportunities." However, she "felt very strongly about it, so [she] was able to stand up for [herself]."

Many genderless kei agree that their clothing has little to do with their sexuality. As Masafumi Monden, researcher of Japanese fashion and culture and the University of Technology Sydney, states, "In Japan, how people look and their sexual identities can be separated to a certain extent." This statement does not hold entirely true, in terms of an outsider's point of view, as Toman had often been asked about his sexuality when wearing genderless clothing; however, by engaging in the culture, these people have allowed themselves the opportunity to question, and, in some cases, shed their prejudices.

These models and idols provide insight into the mindset and daily lives of the Japanese people that reject the existing gender constructs, and perhaps represent the ideology of a larger group in the works.

Backlash

There continues to be pushback against challengers to the social norm. For example, in an interview by Ask-Japanese, an effeminate-dressing student from Bunka College of Fashion states that during his everyday life, on the train and on his way to school, people give him weird looks, and he wishes they would stop. In a different interview, Toman agrees, adding, "We are shamed by a lot of people... People see me wearing makeup and say it's gross."

Toman states: "[Japan] holds on to old customs of telling men and women to be a certain way. Old people tell me not to dress the way that I do." In fact, in the study, Negotiating What's 'Natural': Persistent Domestic Gender Role Inequality in Japan, Scott North measures gender ideology with responses to the statement "Men should work outside and women should protect the household." In comparison with their younger counterparts, of which 59.3% of males and 65.9% of females disagree, the Japanese elders lean towards maintaining the status quo with this traditional line of thinking, with 66.1% of males 60.7% of females in agreement.

Harajuku and Shibuya stand out as cities where people are free to express themselves and their sexuality. Those who live in the rural parts of Japan, as another Bunka student states, "don't have a system to accept [those who defy gender norms]." The pressure to conform takes stronger precedence in these regions, allowing for less self-expression.

Why does genderlessness exist in Japan?

Toman's agent, Takashi Marumoto, states of Japanese culture: "There is strong societal pressure to take the standard route, which is to go to a good college and get a good job... The more mainstream and normalized [the genderless kei] become, the more people will be inspired to live true to themselves."

A major societal criticism from genderless kei is that nowadays males are scolded for wearing skirts while females can wear both pants and skirts. Junko Mitsuhashi, 61, adjunct lecturer in gender studies at Meiji university and a transgender woman, elaborates, "In my generation, women were jealous of men because they could work and do whatever they wanted. In the younger generation, men are jealous of women because they can express themselves through fashion."

Future Implications

For some, to be genderless is an exploration into fashion and self-love only. For others, it includes sexuality and opportunity for those questioning their gender to safely explore. While there remains little discussion around the topic of genderlessness on its own currently, an overall community is being built.

Ranma Yuu, actress and dancer, describes: "There is a clothing boutique that my friend owns. It's where genderless, unisex, and people who like fashion hang out and form a community." More genderless boutiques have cropped up, in addition, such as San To Nibu No Ichi, which is located in Harajuku. Online, Japanese social media is dominated by the presence of a genderless community, as evidenced by the hashtag jendaresu-kei.

The genderless kei are the forerunners in the Japanese expansion into the nonbinary, hoping to establish a culture, as Toman says, "so widespread... that before long it's going to be considered totally normal."

Eunice Lee
Second Place, Nonfiction
"When a Mommy Becomes a Nanny"
Grade 10, Seoul International School
Seoul, South Korea

As a daughter, student, and woman myself, emotional turmoil and rights that are not protected for female Overseas Filipino Workers grieved me the most but impassioned me at the same time. Difficult choices these women had to make, such as being separated from her husband or recently born child, were only the tip of the iceberg in my research. The combined impact of the nation's political strategies, economic fluctuations, and breaking cultural legacy has been shaking the lives of woman in the Philippines.

My research for the Writing for Peace Contest gave me an opportunity not only to delve deeply into the culture of my friend but also to reexamine the culture of mine as a Korean. As Korea also went through an accelerated industrial development in the 70s and economic crisis in the 90s, I was encouraged to compare how two different cultures formed themselves through such difficulties in utterly different manners. The role of women in different positions of the culture, lifestyles of international migrants in the society, and psychological health of adolescent in relation to their parents drew my attention.

Looking at artists' photographs gave me great insight throughout my research. For example, Xyan Cruz Bacani, an artist who I found through this research, used to work as a Filipino domestic helper at Hong Kong herself. She recently started recording her life as a female migrant worker and stories of other helpers inside Hong Kong in black and white photographs. I have always enjoyed reading in all kind of different formats, whether it be books, online articles, magazines, or databases. However, her visual art gave me resonating sympathy and emotion at a different level.

When a Mommy Becomes a Nanny

With her left forefinger, Pamela was carving her daughter's name "Tala" into the snow. "This is my first time to see the snow," she murmured. "It never snows in Philippines."

In Philippines, approximately forty percent of households have an Overseas Filipino Worker (OFW) family member. It is quite common for parents and children in the Philippines to live apart. Children live with an aunt or grandmother because his/her mother works as a nanny in Hong Kong and father works as a seaman in Alaska. With a long history of over forty years, the idea of Filipinos working overseas had become established in the 1970s to serve as a rather impetuous solution for soaring unemployment rate and balance of payments crisis. Under the military dictatorship of Ferdinand Marcos over twenty years the policies encouraging the export of human labor got established, embedded, and rapidly increased surpassing the Asian economic crisis in 1990s.

Mom told me that Pamela and I first met soon after I turned three. Both of my parents were working in New York back then and they needed someone who can take care of me during their absence. My parents found Pamela through a broker and luckily they were fond of each other instantly. Mom liked Pamela because she used to be a teacher back in the Philippines. "I was a very lucky one to meet your parents," Pamela said. "I left the Philippines when my Tala turned three and I met you when you were three."

According to the Philippine Statistics Authority, in 2018 alone, the number of OFWs was estimated at 2.3 million and percentage of female workers surpassed male workers, comprising about 55.8 percent of the total. In the early stage of its OFW migration policies, the Philippine government received positive reviews from the international community. However, it gradually created criticisms inside the Philippines and eventually from the international organizations, such as United Nation and European Union, because the Philippine government's overseas employment strategy has caused unimaginable costs on the workers, whose rights were often not fully protected while abroad.

How tall is she? Does she hate cucumber like me? Don't you miss her? All the questions that I asked Pamela innocently and sincerely out of curiosity must had hurt her so much. "Tala goes to the best preschool in my hometown." Pamela seemed very proud and relieved. She also told me that her family back home could buy a cow after her working for my parents in about two years. The morning after her payday, Pamela always went to the bank to wire everything she earned back to the Philippines.

About 2.56 million children in Philippines have one or both parents working overseas. One of the major reasons for an OFW to decide to go abroad is the advantages his/her children will have economically, academically, and medically. However, the presence of a mother is postponed indefinitely as a cost of economic gain, and the time that would have been spent taking care of her children is used for watching over the employer's children. Undocumented migrant workers do not even have the option to travel back to the Philippines to see their children. Majority of female OFW "bear a lot of guilt in leaving their children behind, and the fact that they care for other children while they leave their own in the care of others haunts them."

"Ina (mother in Filipino), Find her! Now! You are supposed to take care of her so I can work without any worries and send money! What if she is kidnapped and never come back home!" Pamela rarely got upset or raised her voice. But that specific day, she looked like a crazy, insane, simply another person. Right the next day, Pamela went back to the Philippines. Tala was missing. And my vague memory of Pamela completely stops there.

"Children have different levels of acceptance or tolerance, depending on their cognitive development." Infant and preschool children may accept their overseas working parents' migration as a form of abandonment, especially when they are apart from their mothers. Adolescent and teenagers, on the other hand, could understand the situation and either be receptive or rather resentful of their parents. The rate of acceptance varies depending on the age. Such complex challenges and difficulties strike migrant parents and their children every day, constantly.

When I met Pamela again after more than ten years, fragments of my childhood memories burst out from somewhere inside of me. Pamela only recently restarted to work as an OFW again and happened to be designated in Seoul by the employment administration. There she decided to contact my parents to make an old apology regarding herself quitting and leaving her job so suddenly without any notice more than ten years ago. Pamela did not mention anything about Tala.

Traveling overseas for working opportunities and then migration back to the Philippines has become a cycle for OFWs, as they experience insufficient economic opportunities every time they return home. In the year 2016 alone, approximately 10 million OFWs all over the world remitted at least $29 billion back to the Philippines.

When the issues of OFWs are examined, often politics, labor, money, or GDP gets the most attention. However, it is rather the OFW's collection of family and love stories that indeed requires more consideration. Among them exist the heartrending stories of family separation and bond, conflicting duties and loyalties, and difficulties of providing material and emotional needs under a big umbrella of global economy. The Philippine government's oversea employment program has offered immediate work opportunities for the workers and enabled secure economic future for the worker's families left behind. However, the exodus of Philippine workers to close by or faraway countries caused almost half of the Philippine families to become dispersed families with greater consequences. What has been practiced solely for the family has been threatening the fundamental root and core meaning of the family.

Junwon Lee
Third Place, Nonfiction
"The Small but Mighty Survivors"
Grade 11, Cheongna Dalton School
Seoul, South Korea

"I was devastated when I read about the aftermath of the 2004 tsunami in Thailand and the broken families it left behind. Reading about how survivors toiled to rebuild their own lives, uplift others, and continuously honor their lost loved ones was awe-inspiring.

"My research and volunteer experience with the children of Yaowawit School humbled me. Though I complain often, I realize that life in Seoul is comfortable and easy compared to the lives of orphaned children I worked with. Seeing them smile despite their bleak circumstances taught me that I can actively choose react positively to negative situations. I believe I should use the resources easily available to me in South Korea to better the lives of the disadvantaged.

"Drawing from my own personal experience was the most helpful for composing this essay. The unforgettable and priceless first-hand experience granted me with invaluable memories that served as a great help in writing this essay."

The Small but Mighty Survivors at Yaowawit

I didn't know gratitude until the school's one old electric generator sputtered to life again, flooding my cramped room in Yaowawit with light. While my eyes adjusted after being in darkness for several hours, I heard shouts of joy from other volunteers as they praised the heavens for clean water rushing from the communal drinking faucet. It was only my second day volunteering with the Yaowawit School in Kapong, Thailand, and I'd already developed a newfound appreciation for steady access to electricity and drinkable water.

Located in Phang Nga province of Southern Thailand, Kapong is a densely wooded province that almost never makes it to any traveler's bucket list. Unlike the resort-studded tourist mecca Phuket, just two hours south, the atmosphere of Kapong is quieter and gentler. The ocean is not overrun with boats and jetskis; nightclubs are few; the tropical sunset goes uninterrupted by colossal shopping malls. Although the area was greatly affected after a devastating tsunami in 2004 that killed thousands, it is still known for its temple-studded landscape and waterfalls and hiking trails at Khao Lak-Lumru National Park. Years after the tsunami, Kapong is once again teeming with life and local flavor.

Established in 2006, the Yaowawit School doubles as an orphanage for children who have been affected by the tsunami, poverty, or have been abandoned by their parents. The 138 children currently housed there receive a proper Thai education, English language classes, and personal development and enrichment. The nearest convenience store is miles away, so the school is self-sustaining with farms and fishing ponds that the children work themselves.

Seeing children no older than ten vigorously working the land with their callused hands made me hyper-aware of the soft, sensitive skin of my own palm. I was supposed to be older and wiser, but the children made me feel astonishingly young. Some had lost their families to tsunamis or were rescued from human trafficking; it seemed as if they had lived so many lives already. How could they smile while planting banana trees when life had been so unfair?

It was ironic that I was there to assist and mentor the children when they clearly had grasped a concept of life that I hadn't mastered. Still, as a mentor, it was part of my job to lead English language classes and hold counseling sessions for the children. I became close with one particular student named Que (pronounced Kew), who never missed any of my sessions. He was sold twice by his parents, who were poor and couldn't afford to care for him properly. When he returned home for the second time, his parents dropped him off at Yaowawit. His smile lit up the English classroom. He hung onto my every word during our sessions and tackled every task with the same attention and earnesty. It was as if he was unphased by his past troubles and his life at Yaowawit was the only one that mattered.

When I visited his house later in the summer, we had to walk through a dense forest for two hours. There was no proper road because Kapong is one of two provinces not connected by the highway that ran the length of Phang Nga, so we struggled to make our way through bumps, overgrown roots, snakes, and low-hanging willows. Once we got there, we were invited into a tiny, roof-less wooden shack with holes in its walls. In the far corner of the room, a misshapen figure was lying on its side. It was Que's dad. He had slipped during the rainy season and hurt his back. Because the family was poor, they couldn't afford the proper medical attention, so all they could do was watch Que's dad groan in excruciating pain for days, until his entire back took on an abnormal and twisted shape.

I'd expected Que to be angry with his parents when he saw them again. I know I would be if my parents had sold me twice. I'd been angry at my parents for much less severe offenses. But Que greeted his parents and the rest of his family cheerfully and zipped around the house to start his chores. The other volunteers and I followed his lead. We washed clothes in an old bucket and gathered resources from the forest for the family to use. At every turn, I was met with the father's smiling face of approval. He said something in Khmer then to the translator that had come with us. The translator said, "He says that he's very happy you're here to help."

It was easy to see where Que's resilience came from. Here was his father, who had been dealt an unfair hand, and a debilitating injury to boot, thanking me for something as small as doing daily chores. I didn't do much. I didn't fix holes in the wall, heal his injury, or change their lives in a substantial way. I could only help that once. In the following days, the family would have to complete these tasks alone, but they appreciated that their load was a little lighter on that one day. In that moment I realized how powerful and uplifting gratitude can be.

The realization was followed by shame at my own privilege. In Seoul, I'd been annoyed at my parents for being overbearing. I complained about the heat when I had air conditioning or cursed when there was no wifi. My worries all seemed so trivial in comparison to theirs. By spending time with Que and his family, I learned that the decision to be happy is an immensely personal one, separate from one's circumstances. I hadn't met anyone else in my life who faced harder challenges than the Khmer people of Thailand, nor anyone with deeper gratitude or brighter smiles.

Contributors

POETRY

Jee-Won M. E. Arkoi, 19 years old, is a Librian who enjoys reading contemporary poetry, memoirs, and other literary materials that appeal to people's emotions. She is a junior student of Social Work at Stella Maris Polytechnic, Mother Pattern College of Health Sciences, and aspires to become a Psychologist. Jee-Won writes poetry as a way of telling her story and she benefits from the mentorship of Dr. Patricia Jabbeh Wesley through the Young Scholars of Liberia program in Monrovia, Liberia.

Pilar Rodriguez Aranda is a poet, video artist, and translator. She was born in Mexico City, but lived in California, Texas, and New Mexico, for a total of 13 years; currently she resides in Tijuana, BC.

She has published in dozens of magazines and anthologies like *Voices of Mexico, Poets in Nigeria, Mujeres de Maíz, The America's Review, Bilingual Review* and *Voces sin fronteras,* to mention a few. Her published work includes: *Asunto de mujeres* (2012), *Verdes Lazos* (2014), *Diálogos de una Mujer Despierta,* 12 poems set to original live music (2016), *Insistencia en el sueño* (2018), and the bilingual eBook, *Una familia más* (2018), available in all digital platforms. Pilar has been part of several poetry conferences and festivals in Mexico, Brasil, Ecuador, Italy, Cuba and Egypt; her work has been translated into English, Arabic, Greek, Italian, Portuguese and German.

As a video artist she has received awards and grants; a retrospective exhibit of some her work is programmed to be shown at the Cineteca in Madrid this coming fall.

Maureen Jennifer Davies is a 19-year old Liberian student, studying Biology and Chemistry at Stella Maris Polytechnic, Mother Pattern College of Health Sciences. She resides in Monrovia with her parents and two siblings. She wants to become a medical doctor and writer, and is a member of Young Scholars of Liberia under the mentorship of Dr. Patricia Jabbeh Wesley.

Mary Carroll-Hackett is the author of eight collections of poetry: *The Real Politics of Lipstick, Animal Soul, If We Could Know Our Bones, The Night I Heard Everything, Trailer Park Oracle, A Little Blood, A Little Rain,* and *Death for Beginners,* released from Kelsey Books in October 2017. Her newest chapbook, *(Un)Hinged,* was just released Spring 2019. Mary teaches in the Creative Writing programs at Longwood University and with the low-residency MFA faculty at West Virginia Wesleyan. Mary is currently at work on a novel.

After military service, **William Conelly** took both Bachelor's and Master's Degrees in English at the University of California, Santa Barbara. Unrelated writing and research followed, before he returned to academia. Since 2000, Conelly has served in both America and the UK as an associate professor, tutor and seminar leader in writing and English Studies. Retired, now he resides in the West Midlands town of Warwick. In 2015 The Able Muse Press published an assortment of Conelly's verse titled *Uncontested Grounds*; it may be reviewed at their website or via Amazon.

Elaine Gerard has been writing poetry and short stories since the age of 12. Born as a member of the Blackfeet Tribe, Elaine grew up in northern Montana and spent many of her adult years on the Navajo reservation in Arizona. Elaine's poetry has appeared in *Haight Ashbury Literary Journal, Red Ink,* and *Yellow Medicine Review*, among others. Her book of collected poems is *NDN: the words of a little hawk*, published by Poetic Justice Press. She enjoys painting, beadwork, and sewing in her spare time. Elaine resides in beautiful Spokane, Washington, with her partner and his daughter.

Veronica Golos is the author of the poetry books, *Rootwork: Lost Writings of John Brown and Mary Day Brown* (3: A Taos Press), *Vocabulary of Silence* (Red Hen Press, 2011), winner of the 2011 New Mexico Book Award, poems from which are translated into Arabic by poet Nizar Sartawi, and *A Bell Buried Deep* (Storyline Press, 2004), co-winner of the 16th Annual Nicholas Roerich Poetry Prize, adapted for stage and performed at Claremont School of Theology, Claremont, CA. Golos has lectured at Columbia University's Teacher's College, Hunter College, Julliard School of Music, Regis University, University of New Mexico, Dine Technical College, Kansas State University, and Colorado State University; she is co-editor of the *Taos Journal of International Poetry & Art*, former Poetry Editor for the *Journal of Feminist Studies in Religion*, and core faculty at Tupelo Press's Writers Conferences. Selections from her upcoming poetry book, *GIRL*, was awarded the international Naji Naaman Honor Prize 2019 out of Beirut, Lebanon. Golos lives in Taos, New Mexico with her husband, David Pérez.

Carol Griffin writes poetry to explore life circumstance, both inner and outer. She is fascinated with how poems can transform us, delving into what it means to be human and our potential to move toward peace. Carol has been published in the *Marin Poetry Center Anthology* and *Birdland Journal.*

Laurel O. Iloani is a university student and a member of Young Scholars of Liberia. He fully participated in all of the Young Scholars of Liberia workshops conducted by Dr. Patricia Jabbeh Wesley in 2018 and 2019, and is an aspiring writer.

D.R. James has taught college writing, literature, and peace-making for 35 years and lives in the woods outside Saugatuck, Michigan. Poetry and prose appear in various journals and anthologies, and his latest of eight poetry collections are *If god were gentle* (Dos Madres) and *Surreal Expulsion* (The Poetry Box).

Antonia Alexandra Klimenko was first introduced on the BBC and to the literary world by the legendary James Meary Tambimuttu of Poetry London–-publisher of T.S. Eliot, Dylan Thoma, Henry Miller and Bob Dylan, to name a few. After his death, it was his friend, the late great Kathleen Raine, who took an interest in her writing and encouraged her to publish. Although her manuscript was orphaned upon "Tambi's" passing, her poems and correspondence have been included in his Special Collections at Northwestern University. A former San Francisco Poetry Slam Champion, Klimenko is widely published. Her work has appeared in (among others) *XXI Century World Literature* (in which she represents France) and *Maintenant : Journal of Contemporary Dada Writing and Art* archived at the Smithsonian Institution in Washington, D.C. and New York's Museum of Modern Art. She is the recipient of two grants: one from Poets in Need, of which Michael (100 Thousand Poets for Change) Rothenberg is a co-founder; the second—the 2018 Generosity Award bestowed on her by Kathleen Spivack and Josheph Murray for her outstanding service to international writers through SpokenWord Paris where she is Writer/ Poet in Residence.

Laurie Kolp is the author of the complete poetry collection, *Upon the Blue Couch,* and chapbook, *Hello, It's Your Mother*. Her publications include *Southern Poetry Anthology VIII: Texas, Stirring, Rust + Moth, Whale Road Review, Front Porch Journal,* and more. Laurie lives in Southeast Texas with her husband, three children and two dogs.

Whether with words, camera, or canvas, **Paula Dawn Lietz's** work reflects a broad spectrum of awareness that can be stark and cutting, or warm and expansive. Her work reveals a love of nature, of light and shadows, unique angles and perspectives. She pushes through artistic boundaries, demonstrating a multi-media approach to voice, point-of-view and empathy.

Lian Zi Liu was born in Beijing, and grew up in a family of musicians. She moved to California at the age of nine, and now lives in Pacifica CA with her husband and daughter. A designer by trade and an artist by heart, she turned to writing after the birth and open heart surgery of her daughter. She's been attending poetry workshops at the Writing Salon in San Francisco CA.

Lennart Lundh is a poet, short-fictionist, historian, and photographer. His work has appeared internationally since 1965.

Professor of English and Creative Writing at Lock Haven University, **Marjorie Maddox** has published 11 collections of poetry—including *Transplant, Transport, Transubstantiation* (Yellowglen Prize)—the prose collection *What She Was Saying* (Fomite); children's books; *Common Wealth: Contemporary Poets on Pennsylvania* (co-editor; PSU Press); *Presence* (assistant editor); and 550+ stories, essays, and poems in journals and anthologies. www.marjoriemaddox.com

Djelloul Marbrook is the author of ten books of fiction and twelve of poetry, including *Far from Algiers* (2008, Kent State University Press), winner of the Wick Poetry Prize and the International Book Award in poetry. His latest fiction is the trilogy *Light Piercing Water* (November 2018). His latest is *Suffer the Children* (poems and prose). A retired newspaper editor, photographer and U.S. Navy veteran who grew up in Brooklyn, Long Island and Manhattan, he lives in Germantown with his wife Marilyn. He is widely published in journals and maintains a lively presence on Flickr, Twitter and Facebook (www.facebook.com/djelloul.marbrook.5).

Sandra McGarry is a former elementary school teacher who resides in Colorado. She loves the mountains but gives more preference to the ocean having grown up in the east. She has published in Pilgrimage and Colorado Life Magazine.

Suzanne Ondrus is a Fulbright Scholar in Burkina Faso. Her 2014 book *Passion Seeds*, won the Vernice Quebodeaux prize. She was *Reed Magazine's* Markham 2013 Prize winner in Poetry. Her recent work is in *Visitant* and in *S/tick*. In 2017 she participated in Guinee Conakry's UNESCO World Book Capital.

Carl "Papa" Palmer of Old Mill Road in Ridgeway, Virginia, lives in University Place, Washington. He is retired from the military and Federal Aviation Administration (FAA) enjoying life now as "Papa" to his grand descendants and being a Franciscan Hospice volunteer. Carl is a Pushcart Prize and Micro Award nominee. MOTTO: Long Weekends Forever!

Simon Perchik is an attorney whose poems have appeared in Partisan Review, Forge, Poetry, Osiris, The New Yorker and elsewhere. His most recent collection is The Gibson Poems published by Cholla Needles Arts & Literary Library, 2019. For more information including free e-books and his essay "Magic, Illusion and Other Realities" please visit his website at www.simonperchik.com.

Born in Antigua, West Indies, **Althea Romeo-Mark** is an educator and writer who grew up in St. Thomas, US Virgin Islands. She has lived and taught in St. Thomas, Virgin Islands, USA, Liberia, England, and in Switzerland since 1991. Her poems have been published internationally.

Robin Talbert grew up in North Carolina in the foothills of Appalachia. She has been an attorney for low income people, an advocate for older persons, and a consultant for nonprofits. She is on the board of HelpAge International, a global network. Her poetry has been published in *Passager, Stoneboat, Healing Muse*, and elsewhere. This poem was inspired by the painting "Azure Sky" by Sabiha Iqbal.

Susan Taylor is from Dartmoor in South Devon and has been writing poetry for a long while. She has eight published poetry collections, the latest, *Temporal Bones*, appeared from Oversteps Books. One of her hopes is to bring more radical thinking into a conservative rural community... and she has produced a cabaret for 100 Thousand Poets for Change for the past four years. Her website is www.susantaylor.co.uk

Poet, Cutthroat editor and Black Earth Institute Fellow, **Pam Uschuk** has published seven poetry collections include *CRAZY LOVE* (American Book Award) and *BLOOD FLOWER*, Wings Press, 2015 Book List Notable Book. Translated into more than a dozen languages, her work appears in 300+ journals and anthologies, including Poetry, *Agni Review*, and *Ploughshares*, and her awards include New Millenium Poetry Prize, Best of the Web, Struga International Prize for a theme poem, Dorothy Daniels Writing Award (National League of American PEN Women), and others. Editor of *CUTTHROAT, A JOURNAL OF THE ARTS*, Uschuk also edited the anthology, *Truth To Power: Writers Respond To The Rhetoric Of Hate And Fear*, 2017 and was Guest Editor of *About Place Journal* (aboutplacejournal.org) in 2019. She lives in Tucson, Arizona and Bayfield, Colorado. Her newest collection, *REFUGEE*, will be published by Red Hen Press.

Hardarshan Singh Valia is an Earth Scientist. His work has appeared in journals such as *River babble, Poetic Medicine, Who Writes Short Shorts, Sage-ing, Northwest Indiana Literary Journal, Wards Literary Journal* and the forthcoming anthology entitled *'Dreamscapes'* by Cherry House Press. This poem emerged after reading the news of a boat carrying refugees sank in the ocean.

Guest editor **Patricia Jabbeh Wesley** is a Liberian civil war survivor who immigrated to the United States with her family during the fourteen year Liberian civil war. Her books include *When the Wanderers Come Home, Where the Road Turns, The River is Rising, Becoming Ebony, Before the Palm Could Bloom: Poems of Africa,* and one children's book, *In Monrovia, the River Visits the Sea*. Her poem, "One Day: Love Song for Divorced Women" was featured by US Poet Laureate, Ted Kooser in American Life in Poetry June 13, 2011 edition. Some of her awards include a 2016 WISE Women Award and the Crab Orchard Award. Her poems have appeared in *New Orleans Review, Crab Orchard Review, Prairie Schooner,* among others, and have been translated into several languages. She is an Associate Professor of English and Creative Writing at Penn State University.

Georgia Wilder writes poetry and short fiction. She is a winner of Quattro Books "Best New Poets in Canada" (2018) for her collection *Atom-Bomb Nostalgia*. Her story "Cocoa Divine and the Lightning Police" was nominated for the Journey Prize and appears in the 2015 Journey Prize anthology. She runs a monthly poetry salon in Toronto called Wild Writers, and has featured at many poetry events. She teaches at the University of Toronto.

FICTION

Mike Bates is a former corporate attorney, recently retired to put some context back into his life. His work has appeared in Journals as diverse as Mobius, The Journal of Social Change, The Doctor T. J. Eckleburg Review, and Gadfly Online. He lives with his wife and dog on the north Oregon coast.

William Cass has had over 175 short stories accepted for publication in a variety of literary magazines. His children's book, Sam, is scheduled for release by Upper Hand Press in April 2020. Recently, he received a couple of Pushcart nominations and won writing contests at *Terrain.org* and *The Examined Life Journal*. He lives in San Diego, California.

Edward D. Currelley is an author and artist. His writing is presently on exhibit at The Hudson Valley Museum of Contemporary Art. Publications include *HVCCA Anthology, Between I & Thou, Mom Egg Review, Sling Magazine* and *Metaphor Magazine #5*. He is also a contributor to the online publication *The Peace Correspondent*. His poem, "I America," appears in *Split This Rock*, as part of their Poems of Resistance, Power & Resilience. He received honorable status by *Writer's Digest* for stage playwriting. He is also a Pushcart Prize Nominee. He is the author of two children's books. His recently completed collection of short stories, *Righteous Indignation*, and collection of poems, *Hieroglyphs,* will be published in 2019. He resides in New York City.

Robert Kostuck is an M.Ed. graduate from Northern Arizona University. Recently published fiction, essays, and reviews appear or are forthcoming in *Kenyon Review, The Massachusetts Review, The Southwest Review, Louisiana Literature, Free State Review, Zone 3, Saint Ann's Review, Bryant Literary Review, Concho River Review, Flyway: A Literary Review, Clackamas Literary Review, Silk Road, Fifth Wednesday Journal, Crab Creek Review, Takahē Magazine, Roanoke Review, EVENT*, and *Tiferet*. He is currently working on short stories, essays, and novels. He lives near an ocean; his heart belongs to the Chihuahua and Sonora deserts.

NONFICTION

After hitchhiking around the country in 1966, Vicki Lindner traveled to 39 countries in Latin America, Europe, India, Asia and Africa, often alone. These trips inspired many essays, memoirs, and short fiction which were published in magazines and journals ranging from Cosmopolitan to Ploughshares. As she finishes up a 'sixties memoir, Baby, It's You, she teaches at Lighthouse Writers Workshop, and divides her time between Denver and Leadville, Colorado. She has been an adviser to Writing for Peace since its inception. A recent short story appeared in The Bryant Literary Review.

Anna Redsand is a white, cis-gender lesbian, raised by fundamentalist missionaries in the Navajo Nation. Her most recent book is a memoir, *To Drink from the Silver Cup*. Her essays have appeared in literary journals; "Naturalization" was notable in *Best American Essays 2014*. She lives and writes on the road.

Art & Photography

Elaine Gerard has been writing poetry and short stories since the age of 12. Born as a member of the Blackfeet Tribe, Elaine grew up in northern Montana and spent many of her adult years on the Navajo reservation in Arizona. Elaine's poetry has appeared in *Haight Ashbury Literary Journal, Red Ink,* and *Yellow Medicine Review*, among others. Her book of collected poems is *NDN: the words of a little hawk*, published by Poetic Justice Press. She enjoys painting, beadwork, and sewing in her spare time. Elaine resides in beautiful Spokane, Washington, with her partner and his daughter.

Aaron Ireland is a social entrepreneur, feminist advocate, and motivational speaker, and photographer. Aaron is a mentee mentor of Young Scholars of Liberia who has been with Young Scholars of Liberia since 2018. He recently graduated with a degree in Sociology and Economics.

Whether with words, camera, or canvas, **Paula Dawn Lietz's** work reflects a broad spectrum of awareness that can be stark and cutting, or warm and expansive. Her work reveals a love of nature, of light and shadows, unique angles and perspectives. She pushes through artistic boundaries, demonstrating a multi-media approach to voice, point-of-view and empathy.

Laura Matthias Bendoly is photographer and author whose most recent novel is the age-of-discovery adventure, *The Peddler of Wisdom*. Laura lives in Ohio with her husband and two children. When not writing, she is behind the camera lens, cycling, hiking, and discovering maps, old books, and art catalogs for character inspiration. See more of Laura's photography at http://www.laurabendoly.com/ and browse her fiction titles at https://laurambendoly.wordpress.com and https://www.facebook.com/LauraMatthiasBendoly/

Carmel Mawle is founder of the nonprofit literary organization, Writing for Peace, and has served as Editor-in-Chief of DoveTales, An International Journal of the Arts since 2013. A Pushcart Nominee, her short stories, essays and poetry have been published in literary journals and anthologies, including Smokelong Quarterly and Shake the Tree Anthology.

Vermon Washington is interested in youth development. He is passionate about education for young people. He loves writing and photography, is highly interested in the Fine Arts, and is a student of Stella Maris Polytechnic in Monrovia. He is a member of Dr. Patricia Jabbeh Wesley's Young Scholars of Liberia program in Monrovia, Liberia.

Acknowledgements

Thank you for supporting Writing for Peace through the purchase of our 2019 DoveTales Anthology. We are deeply grateful to all our Panel of Advisers. To our young writers, summit participants, and the many artists who contributes their stories, poems, art and photography. We thank you for entrusting your work with us.

Many thanks to our Board of Directors for their leadership and tireless efforts on behalf of Writing for Peace.

We are grateful to Longwood University for their valuable sponsorship, and all our generous contributors.

Last, but not least, we would like to thank our esteemed Adviser and Guest Editor, Dr. Patricia Jabbeh Wesley, for dedicating much of her busy summer to our first online edition of DoveTales. She did this while inspiring her Young Scholars of Liberia, and we are so grateful to have the opportunity to appreciate the work of these talented young people.

Writing for Peace is a 501c3 nonprofit corporation (Federal Tax ID Number, 45-2968027). Your donations make this endeavor possible.

www.ingramcontent.com/pod-product-compliance
Lightning Source LLC
Chambersburg PA
CBHW061030120726
47910CB00006B/2179

* 9 7 8 0 9 8 9 1 2 0 6 7 8 *